Greenville College Library

Presented by:
Dr. J. David Fairbanks

977.31.   G76

D1172653

LORDS
OF
THE LAST
MACHINE

977.31
G76

LORDS
OF
THE LAST
MACHINE

THE STORY
OF POLITICS IN
CHICAGO

**Bill Granger
and
Lori Granger**

RANDOM HOUSE

NEW YORK

Copyright © 1987 by Granger & Granger, Inc.
All rights reserved under International
and Pan-American Copyright Conventions.
Published in the United States by
Random House, Inc., New York, and
simultaneously in Canada by
Random House of Canada Limited, Toronto.

Library of Congress Cataloging-in-Publication Data

Granger, Bill.
Lords of the last machine.

Includes index.
1. Chicago (Ill.)—Politics and government—1951—2. Daley, Richard J.,
1902–1976. I. Granger, Lori. II. Title.
F548.52.G73   1987   977.3'11043
86-29637
ISBN 0-394-54238-X

Manufactured in the
United States of America

First Edition

TITLE PAGE PHOTOGRAPHS
BY BETSY WEISS VAN DIE

TYPOGRAPHY AND BINDING DESIGN
BY BARBARA M. BACHMAN

This book is dedicated to all political pros
who develop their skills with proper
amounts of cynical fairness and a
skeptical lack of bias.

This is for the late Dr. Milton Rakove and
the late Ralph Berkowitz—friends in the
political games we all played.

116706

Politics is about money.

—F. RICHARD CICCONE

CONTENTS

LORDS
OF
THE LAST
MACHINE

The Center Does Not Hold

THERE IS AN ELEGANT CHICAGO THAT AMBLES GRACEFULLY from the Sears Tower on the southwest boundary of the downtown section up across the Chicago River to the John Hancock Center on Michigan Avenue. It is a glittering thing that takes in theaters, opera, symphony orchestra, museums and horse-drawn hansom cabs that clip-clop down the early evening streets. That elegant city continues north of the Hancock building on into the gracious neighborhoods of re-habilitated homes and elegant high rises along the miles of Lincoln Park, from Old Town north and west.

In this Chicago, there are men and women who control empires across the world and who enjoy an ambience that is both comfortable and charming, that has wit and a certain cynical tolerance that accepts the world for the sorry thing it is and tries to make it better. This Chicago remembers its saints, secular and religious, its poets, architects, writers and musicians.

When the citizens of this Chicago wake up in the morning and look out their windows to the east over Lake Michigan or to the west toward miles of suburbs stretching out into flat prairie land, it is an accident of birth or business. This Chicago is like a hundred other such cities which nestle inside the population centers of the United States or of Europe.

There is another Chicago to be found in the neighborhoods that range across the sprawling city, ten miles west and thirty miles north and south. It begins in the shadows of the graceful towers and moves out into the suburbs that interlock into the traffic grid of the core of the old downtown. This other Chicago is a city of brick bungalows and three-flats, where descendants of Eastern European immigrants and African slaves and Irish peasants push and jostle each other for a few rooms to live in, a job, room to breathe.

On these streets of the other Chicago, political ideas are conservative. When religion enters into things, that religion is usually Catholic. And language is blunt, making full use of racial and ethnic labels that may not reflect calculated prejudice so often as a bitter recognition of how things are and how they have always been. When the citizens of this other city speak of the places and loyalties of their lives, their talk is of the neighborhood and not that broader urban conglomeration that includes the elegant Chicago.

The two cities exist side by side, but their points of contact are few. Each can ignore the other—and each does. Each is necessary to the other, but no one considers it quite polite to remark upon that fact.

The politics of Chicago is the creature of that second Chicago, the Chicago of the neighborhoods. That this kind of politics works out ways to satisfy the needs of the other Chicago is proved by its continuation.

In the neighborhoods stand piles of old public school buildings, some more than a century old in a city that is barely fifty years older than that. On all the school buildings, above the dreary concrete playgrounds, are signs that say: No Hard Ball Playing Allowed.

And that is the key to understanding the other Chicago and the political life that springs from it: this city specifies the few areas where hard ball playing is not allowed.

The politics of the neighborhoods is tied to the idea of the ward, the parish church, the block, the school. It has no truck with international culture or national policy. It does not concern itself with things that do not matter—now, today, this week, right here, to my friends and my family. Above everything else it is practical. It speaks of the concrete: the broken sidewalk or the pothole in the street, the contract to be let, the job to be filled.

There are no gracious winners in politics when it is played like this. When you win, your opponent is not beaten: he is eliminated, wiped out, dismembered and sometimes simply killed. No one weeps for the losers (save, perhaps, people in those elegant clubrooms, in leather chairs where people sometimes wonder, over brandy, what ever became of what's-his-name). If you are not going to be a winner, you do not belong in the game at all. It is the first obligation of the winners to show you this.

The winners will clear up your misunderstanding in language that is brutal and simple: they speak clearly of money and contracts and favors, of cutting a deal. They speak of friendship and how friends help each other, and what they mean is that if you are not a friend and you are in the game, then you are an enemy. There is no middle ground. Chicago makes no pretense: politics is about money.

People go into politics to make money. It is no surprise, then, that many become rich in the game. George Dunne, a Machine lord who grew wealthy through his "connected" insurance business, once said, "Anybody who goes into politics for some other reason than making money is a fool."[1]

The names of the big winners are displayed on the streets and expressways and schools and plazas in the larger city, even in the elegant part. Cermak has his road, Dan Ryan has his expressway, Hoyne has his avenue, Daley has his plaza and Petrillo his bandshell.

Chicago politicians save the talk about idealism, about the political good or the commonweal for Fourth of July speeches. No politician would want his constituents to believe he is a fool, as they would if he began to talk about the great issues of the age. A politician in Chicago can always work up an enthusiastic speech on the high quality of garbage pickup in his ward, however.

The language can fall strangely on the ears of outsiders. The talk is a shorthand, but it connects those who understand it. They ask what parish you're from, and even if you are a Jew, you can identify yourself with the Catholic parish you were raised in. They ask who sent you to their office, and you name a sponsor—called a rabbi in New York, but a chinaman in Chicago—and that places you on the scale of favor-seekers. They want to know your "clout" (a Chicago word co-opted by the national press), they want to place you in a hierarchy that is never written down and that shifts from day to day. The pattern inside this politics is as complex as the court of Versailles, and the key to understanding it is simply that politics is about money. If you pretend not to comprehend this or say that the rules might be changed—if you become vaguely philosophical or idealistic—then you are marked as an outsider and shunted away from power.

IF YOU UNDERSTAND A LITTLE ABOUT THE TOUGH, TIGHT, BRU-tal and absolutely confident game of hard ball played in Chicago politics, then you can understand what happened at the end of August 1968, when the Democrats played their last convention in the city.

When Abbie Hoffman and Rennie Davis and Jerry Rubin came to Chicago, it was as though Marco Polo had stumbled into the court of the Great Khan and told him that China was not the Middle Kingdom and center of the world.

The Chicago Seven—as they and their companions would be called at their trial—did not know the language of the city they would confront. They imagined that politics was about ideas. If Abbie Hoffman had been told that, in Chicago, garbage is politics and politics is garbage, he might have thought it was a joke. To the demonstrators who came, the city was a stage that had been set up by accident when the Democratic National Committee chose it as the site of the convention.

The accident was to tear back the layers of politeness that had shielded the politics of Chicago's neighborhoods from outsiders' eyes. The times were not propitious for quiet and dignity or for the healing of old wounds that had been supposed to go on at the convention. In the months before August, there had been tremors along a faultline that reached into Chicago neighborhoods from the outer world. The pressure had been building all year.

Two years before, in 1966, Martin Luther King, Jr., had come to the city and staged a series of open housing marches in Mayor Richard J. Daley's segregated home neighborhood of Bridgeport and in nearby Cicero. With some aides, he had lived for a time in a West Side ghetto apartment building to demonstrate the plight of poor blacks. Housing was always a critical issue in Chicago, and King understood this: it was a city where blacks and whites might ride the same El trains, eat in the same restaurants, work in the same jobs side by side. But when night came, they went back to separate neighborhoods. Yet despite his national prestige King left Chicago with a claim to victory that was hollow rhetoric. The politicians of Chicago's Machine had simply outwaited him.

King died on April 4, 1968, in Memphis. On April 5, blacks of the West Side of Chicago, a four-mile stretch of neighborhood, went on a rampage, burning down homes, stores and restaurants and shooting at each other and at the police. Before it was over, Mayor Daley, in a rage that had him choking back tears, had ordered police to shoot down anyone caught burning or looting. The riot echoed earlier racial upheavals in the city, but the property damage caused by it outdid anything Chicago had seen before. Twenty years later, most of the West Side that was destroyed that weekend is still rubble. No one will build there.

That same April, a group of middle-class demonstrators for peace, most of them middle-aged white women, marched in the Loop in daylight, on a rainy Saturday, and they were attacked by gangs of policemen, many without uniforms. The police had been ordered to the attack by City Hall, which was reacting in paranoia and frustration against those who might hurt the city and its image. This was the attitude of Chicago's political leaders as they awaited the convention.

What the hard-ball players in the Hall did not understand, or did not wish to understand, was that the rhetoric of confrontation that people like Hoffman delighted in was only talk. Daley and his advisors, not used to this strange, theatrical brand of politics, took the Hoffmans of the world at their word. When the demonstrators announced that they would shut down the city, City Hall scurried to protect itself. And the Daley forces thought the unrelated incidents of the West Side black riots and the peace demonstration were part of some larger plan.

The actors in this political drama did not speak the same language—the Yippies did not understand the importance of precinct captains and garbage can lids, and the Machine did not understand that "up against the wall, motherfuckers" could be just a way of talking.

For weeks before the convention, the demonstrators drifted into the city wearing odd clothes. One afternoon they let loose, in the plaza later named for Richard J. Daley, a pig named Pigasus—a presidential nominee, they said. It was quite a show, and the conservative neighborhoods let their politicians know how much they disapproved.

At the same time, the Chicago press, which was going through a particularly vicious period of circulation war hysteria, covered the coming confrontation with the calm impartiality of an Iranian religious leader.

The *Chicago Daily News* reported with horror that Chicago's drinking water, drawn from Lake Michigan, was to be contaminated with LSD.

The *Chicago American,* lurching luridly from its Hearst past to an early grave in 1974, revealed a plot by demonstrators to assassinate all the major political leaders gathering in Chicago, including Mayor Daley and top members of his administration.

The newspapers agreed that there were at least 100,000 dope-smoking hippies poised to descend upon the helpless city and throw themselves at the barricade of a thin blue line of policemen wearing regulation baby-blue football helmets.

Nineteen sixty-eight had been a year of political madness framing the horror of all that was still happening in Vietnam. It saw the Tet offensive, the assassinations of Robert Kennedy and Martin Luther King, Jr.; it witnessed race riots in scores of cities; and a president announced that he would not run again. If the world was coming apart—and so it seemed to be—then Chicago's anxiety was no worse than anyone else's.

In this atmosphere of hysteria, Richard Daley and the Machine prepared the city to host the national convention. First, there were the police. Twelve thousand Chicago policemen were ordered on twelve-hour shifts and prepared for war with clubs, Mace, guns and bullets. (Amazingly, not one person would be shot or killed in connection with the street violence of that shattering week.)

The Illinois National Guard was summoned to its Chicago Avenue armory and told to wait for orders. (They eventually were deployed, with jeeps and barbed-wire barricades, on Michigan Avenue.) Six thousand army troops were flown into Glenview Naval Air Station, north of the city, on alert. In addition, Illinois state troopers, U.S. Secret Service, FBI agents and private security guards were gathered into the army of defense. About twenty-five thousand men in all eventually were deployed in the city streets, mostly in an area four miles long.

Daley was at the center of the action. He had ordered wooden fences erected to conceal the crumbling side streets that ran between the Conrad Hilton Hotel on South Michigan Avenue and the old International Amphitheatre where the convention was to be held. The delegates seemed nervous, what with the pomp, the military preparations, the edgy mood of the police around the hotel and the demonstrators marching outside. And they did not understand Daley. To this day, some profess not to understand him.

It was really very simple: Chicago was Daley's city because he loved it and because he had won it in the game of hard ball. People who marred Chicago's name picked a fight with Daley. It was that personal.

There were other things, of course: the city's reputation, its need to maintain convention business, to project a positive image and protect its climate for business. For these reasons, too, the demonstrators had to be contained. But more important than these things was the fact that if you insulted his city, you insulted Richard J. Daley. The Democratic Convention was supposed to bring honor to Chicago and, naturally, to Daley. That was, after all, why it was being held in Chicago.

Outsiders caught in the confrontation that week did not understand that the city was defending itself in a traditional way: by attack. It is the only possible defense in the game of politics as it is played in Chicago.

On Sunday night, convention eve, the police were ordered to enforce an 11 P.M. curfew in Lincoln Park where the demonstrators had gathered. It was an order they had been waiting for. They waded into the park, into the bushes and groves and under the elm trees, and they beat at the demonstrators with their billy clubs and gassed them with tear gas. They chased four thousand demonstrators out of the park for defying the curfew, a misdemeanor. Some were thrown into the retention pond. Some were beaten bloody with the hickory-wood sticks.

And the press, the national press, did not understand. Reporters and photographers held out their credentials to the police. The police beat them in answer. Cameras were smashed and reporters from Philadelphia and New York ended up in the hospital.

That the bare brutality of the Chicago police seemed to shock the out-of-town reporters only branded them as part of the enemy. In the eyes of the police, they had chosen their side.

The following day, Monday, Grant Park was the scene of a new confrontation. Against the chanting of the demonstrators, the police moved, chanting their own formula: "Kill, kill, kill." They advanced in ragged lines like doughboys crossing Flanders Fields. At midnight, in Lincoln Park again, the police took off their name tags before they assaulted the human lines formed against them. Twenty newspapermen ended up in hospitals that night.

The horror spread. The week passed in revved-up time, out of synch with reality. Each new day was like a new act of an unending play.

The confrontation of the streets was matched and echoed inside the ancient exposition hall in the Stockyards. On Tuesday a newsman in the hall was punched out by a security guard, and a prominent television reporter was thrown out of the hall, live and on camera.

The delegates staggered through the old convention rituals and procedures for two days, trying to pretend that everything that was happening was not happening. The television cameras studied Daley in the hall with worried fascination: Daley laughing, Daley applauding, Daley conferring with his advisers.

No one understood: when Chicago politicians are attacked—when they feel threatened—they fight back with every means, and they fight to win or die. The outsiders thought a demonstration was just a demonstration. They did not understand that being reasonable about opposition was not a part of the Chicago political tradition.

On Wednesday night in the convention hall, a delegate

from Wisconsin named Donald Peterson stood up and asked for the convention to adjourn for two weeks and open somewhere else. He called the demonstrators on the street "children."

The cameras turned to examine an infuriated Daley. His face became purple, and his son, Richard M., sitting next to him in the Illinois delegation, blushed with rage. You do not use gentle words about your enemies in Chicago.

The next blow came from a Colorado delegate who interrupted the proceedings to say: "Is there any rule under which Mayor Daley can be compelled to suspend the police-state terror being perpetrated at this minute on kids in front of the Conrad Hilton?"

The question set off young Richard, who leaped to his feet, raised his fists in an offer to fight and yelled insults. His reaction energized the immense Illinois delegation—under Daley's control—to do the same. No one could be understood with all the shouting going on. It was just as well: no one would have understood in any case. Chicago politicians were explaining the rules of the game at the tops of their voices: if you are not with us, then you are against us.

The final electric moment in the hall came when the scholarly Abraham Ribicoff, senator from Connecticut, took the rostrum to drumbeat for his candidate, George McGovern. Three days earlier, he had come to Daley and the Illinois delegation and asked them to support McGovern. Now he was on national television saying, "If we had McGovern, we wouldn't have the Gestapo in the streets of Chicago!"

Daley led the delegation of mostly portly men in shiny suits to their feet. He waved his big Irish fist in the air, and his face was full of hate. The television microphones did not pick up his shouts over the general hubbub, but a lip reader employed by an antiestablishment paper in the city said that he said: "Fuck you, you Jew son of a bitch, you lousy mother-fucker, go home."

No one really doubted that he said something like that.

WHAT HAPPENED IN 1968 IN CHICAGO CHANGED THE DEMO-cratic party profoundly. Some believe it may have shattered the party's patched-together Rooseveltian unity so completely that the Democrats are doomed to a long-term role as the party out of national power. Certainly the draconian rule changes in the nomination process engendered by the abuses of 1968 led to the disastrous nomination of McGovern in 1972 and Carter in 1976 (Carter won but it might have been better for the party if he had not).

But what it did to Chicago was more subtle. Though the people who sat on boards and gave balls and collected for charity may have disapproved of what happened on the streets and in the convention hall, the neighborhoods were pleased. The cops had done the right thing; Daley had not faltered. Such was his power in 1968.

The Democratic party limped out of town and the payroll-ers from Streets & Sanitation cleaned up the mess. The out-of-town reporters went home and wrote bitterly about the city. For two decades, planners for political conventions have shunned Chicago, and Chicago has not made a serious bid for a convention in that time.

Daley did not care. He did not limp out of town. He stayed in the game. When the Chicago Seven went on trial, he showed up to testify, and he was smiling and very certain in his testimony. At the beginning, the defense asked him: "What is your name?"

"Richard J. Daley."

"And what do you do?"

"I am mayor of Chicago."

He had carried the city into battle, and he also carried the city for Humphrey and the Democratic ticket in 1968.

A year after the convention, Daley told a crowd, "Someone asked me a few days ago, would you do over what you did in August? And in the true tradition of the Gaelic spirit of the Daleys, I said: 'You're damned right I'd do the same thing, only with greater effort.' "

In 1971, Daley ran for his fifth term as mayor of Chicago. All the newspapers endorsed him. All the civic leaders and art patrons endorsed him, because Chicago was the City That Works and because all around them they saw examples of the beauty, wealth and strength of the city. The business community in the bustling boards of trade on LaSalle Street also endorsed him. And the neighborhoods backed him all the way.

He won 424,000 votes, 70 percent of the total. And the Democrats swept all 50 wards in the city for the first time in history.

Those numbers and the stubborn belligerence of tone in the city that lay behind those numbers—that stemmed not only from the 1968 convention but from everything that had gone before—are the key to understanding the last major city political Machine in the country, how it worked, and why in time it finally fell apart.

1

The City Alone

THE CITY IS SPLENDID IN ISOLATION. IT SITS ALONE ON A swamp a thousand miles west of the great megalopolis along the Atlantic seaboard. The vast prairie stretches west a thousand more miles before it bumps against the bulk of the Rockies.

Chicago looks around and sees nothing like itself. It has tenuous links—by rail and plane and commerce—with New York, whose size and success produce a perpetual braying rivalry that is almost always one-sided.

The bragging never stops: it is small-townish in such a big city and sometimes embarrassing. Brochures issued by the city explaining various summer festivals include the tag line:

"Chicago, a World Class City." City Hall does not understand that world-class cities do not have to describe themselves in this way.

When Chicago and New York both tried to get the Columbian Exposition at the turn of the century, Chicago politicians made such extravagant promises that a New York newspaper editor named Charles Dana called Chicago "the Windy City" for all the hot air coming out of the place. The hot air prevailed, the fair was held. It was the wonder of the age, and it was probably the golden zenith of the city then scarcely sixty years old.

The name Chicago is an Indian word that refers to the stink of wild onions that grew in the swampland that is the site of the city. Chicagoans know this and tell you about it, because of a kind of perverse pride: as Nelson Algren said once, loving Chicago is like loving a woman with a broken nose.

When the Chicago Bears football team ended twenty-two years of frustration by winning the Super Bowl in 1985, its coach Mike Ditka (who has a Chicago face) scored a public relations coup by saying the other team was the kind whose players should all be named Smith and that his team was peopled by "Grabowskis." Chicago loved it; that is the kind of city it is, pretending to lower-class roots and ethnic surnames long after the generations have become gentrified. Even the elegant swells downtown like to think they know how to use the word "ain't."

Chicago assembled itself out of odd lots of immigrants who came on from New York and Boston. The railroads brought them to the Railroad City to work at building more railroads, to work on the killing room floors in the Stockyards or in the immigrant sweatshops and little factories where the Old World languages found their way to an approximate English fusion.

The first people to stick to the spit of land at the juncture of the Chicago River and Lake Michigan were French. The very first settler was an exotic mulatto from Haiti named Jean Baptiste Point du Sable, who set up a fur-trading post about 1772. Around 1800 du Sable decided to move on down the Illinois River, but John Kinzie and François Beaubien continued the trade with the Potawatomi Indians in the neighborhood.

The Chicago pioneers were basically lazy, fun-loving and hard-drinking. Fur trading was a trade that required long periods of idleness as well as practiced chicanery. Success depended on who controlled the business of trading fire-water to the Indians. Chicago had a reputation long before it was a city.

After the French and English traders came American troops, a fort called Dearborn (later destroyed by Indians) and, three decades on, a sudden influx of Germans and then Irish. The Germans and Irish were builders, and a settlement of substance was formed.

IN 1847 BLIGHT STRUCK IRELAND, AND THE POTATOES BEGAN rotting in the fields. It might as well have been a plague that attacked the population: an average adult Irishman of that day ate eleven pounds of potatoes a day and little else.[1] The potato had been brought into Ireland as a cheap way to feed the poor, and it had been such a success that the Irish had forgotten how to eat or cook anything but potatoes. They grew other crops, they raised cattle—but that was for export. When the English and Americans mounted relief efforts and sent them "Indian corn" (maize), it rotted because the Irish had never seen the stuff before and did not know how to cook the grain.

Starvation, sickness and a blistering hatred of the English who presided with dithering futility over the misfortunes of their subject country devastated Ireland. Desperate people made their way onto crammed immigrant ships and fled the disaster that their native land had become. America suddenly received an infusion of English-speaking people touched with genius, bitterness, vigor and intelligence. Their gift of gab and organization became a gift for politics.

The very first Irish had made their way to Chicago before the famine, in 1838, five years after the city was incorporated. They worked on the building of the Illinois and Michigan Canal that arched southwest from the Chicago River and was part of the great river system linking the Mississippi and its tributaries with the Great Lakes. Their first homes were along the river and canal in a neighborhood called Bridgeport, which today lies four miles southwest of the Loop. (The neighborhood was still mostly Irish 120 years later when its most famous son, Richard Joseph Daley, became mayor of Chicago—and he kept living in a Bridgeport bungalow on Lowe Street until his death.)

The city became the rail hub of the country in those years, marking the beginning of a century of decline for St. Louis, the previous "capital" of the Middle West. In the critical decade of railroad growth in the 1840s and 1850s, the Irish population multiplied. Their shanties spread south and west of the Loop on the flatlands and marshes. When canals were built and tracks were laid, the Irish worked for the railroads, particularly the giant Illinois Central that connected the city with the fertile heartland stretching south to New Orleans. The railroads made Chicago a critical link in the west-to-east food chain: live cattle entered the Chicago stockyards and beefsteak went to New York.

Chicago intoxicated the Irish in a way that New York and

Boston did not. The reasons are simple. The city was as raw as the unpainted pine planking on its buildings, a law to itself. It had few patricians. The original settlers had died out and left no mark. The new traders—called merchants—were still building their fortunes and had not yet spent much time worrying about what was proper.

By contrast, New York and Boston were centuries old at this point, and a cold, WASP prejudice against the Irish hordes asserted itself in the "Irish Need Not Apply" signs of the times. The Irish came in at the lowest rung of Chicago society, but it was more a footstool than a stepladder.

ILLINOIS WAS A FREE STATE BY THE SKIN OF ITS TEETH. THE character of the land called Egypt (for its rich river-delta soil) in the southern third of Illinois was rural, agricultural, pioneering and southern, but more akin to the hills of Tennessee and Kentucky than the plantations of Mississippi. Chicago cut a northern mark in the state, but the whole of Illinois— only admitted to the Union in 1818—was more frontier than anything else. As a result, black people were tolerated but not encouraged.

This ambivalent attitude toward blacks—an uneasy neutrality about their existence on the part of native white Americans and the waves of new immigrants—would carry Chicago into a bizarre hypocrisy in culture and politics that still holds sway. It is easy to feel but very hard to put in words.

Example: Chicago schoolchildren into the 1950s were taught that the first settler in Chicago was John Kinzie. In fact, Kinzie was the second settler, although the first white one—du Sable preceded him. A small point, you would think: both were fur traders, and that meant crooks, and both enjoyed reputations that were less than entirely savory. Yet

Chicagoans continue a crazy kind of rivalry in honoring the two reprobates. Was du Sable the first Chicagoan? Or was Kinzie, who created the tradition of the saloonkeeper-politician? And does it matter? It does—but only because one was black and the other white.

Understanding blacks in Illinois history—and, later, in Chicago's—is vital to understanding how the Machine was formed (against the antiethnic union of city WASPS and black Republicans), how it endured (by including blacks as a separate power), and how it fell (riven by black and white factionalism).

Illinois was home to Abraham Lincoln and Stephen A. Douglas at the same time. Douglas, a Democrat, was a man of ambition and eloquence who was a chief supporter of expansion of the Illinois Central railroad. He got around the slavery issue boiling in the country in the 1850s by advocating freedom for free states and letting slave states stay slave.

Illinois was a free state, but—like neighboring Iowa and Indiana—had strict antiblack migration laws. Blacks were not chattel—but they could not vote. Blacks were not slaves—but free blacks had to put up a cash bond to settle in Illinois.

Abraham Lincoln championed the idea of Union above all, and the insistence on the right to own slaves was threatening to shatter the Union. By extension, he was against slavery.

In a remarkable series of debates in the summer of 1858, Lincoln and Douglas rambled about Illinois and engaged in public discussions on the principles of freedom and slavery. They were running against each other for Senator, a position that went to Douglas, even though it is conceded that he lost the great debates. In that summer, Douglas won the Irish over to the Democratic party. The stage was also set for Lincoln's nomination for president by the new Republican party—and for his party's support by enfranchised blacks, support that was to last for decades. (The Lincoln-Douglas debates were suggested by Jesse Fell, great-grandfather of Adlai Stevenson II who became governor of Illinois and ran for President twice in the 1950s.)

The debate over slavery that pitted blacks against Irish in the 1850s was to shape the twentieth-century Democratic party in Chicago as well as the Machine. The conflict was racial and economic. Slavery advocates pointed to the sorry Irish living cheek by jowl in their Chicago shantytowns, scarcely better off than the meanest black plantation slave in Mississippi. The rhetoric of the time spoke of the culture of the Irish in much the same way black culture would be described a century later. The Irish were rural people unused to city life; they lacked education and family stability; they had little control over their emotions; they lived for the present. In short, for their own good they ought to be controlled and protected. Was slavery such a bad system? At least there was security for the slave, as there was none for the scrabbling Irish worker.

The Irish saw the point. They knew that if blacks were free, they would compete with the Irish for low-paying jobs, driving down wages even more. The Irish understood discrimination when it worked against them—their experiences with the English had given them a piercing insight into the rhetorical claims of high-minded people. They also understood how to use discrimination to their own advantage.

And so the Irish aversion to free blacks grew. The Irish flocked to the Democrats for other reasons: Stephen Douglas's wife was a Catholic at a time when Catholicism was ridiculed; the Democrats were more open to immigrants than the native Americans who formed the core of the Whig and later the Republican parties.

Last, the Republican party was founded on the ideology of

Abolition and Union, high-flown concepts that struck the hard-pressed immigrant scratching for a bare living in the new city streets as beside the point.

The lines were very sharp in Chicago. In 1855, the Know-Nothing Party (nativist, naive and anti-Catholic) took over city government and passed a series of draconian social ordinances that interfered with the pleasures of immigrant life, specifically drinking beer.

Beer. Chicago's largest immigrant groups were the Germans and the Irish, and ordinarily they didn't have much use for each other. But the beer issue, in its first notable appearance in Chicago life, had a magical ability to erase past differences. German working men came out of their beer gardens to link arms with Irishmen fired up to save their pubs. The Lager Beer riots that resulted were the earliest example of the Chicagoan's will to fight for the right to drink. Each Sunday was a bloody street brawl from City Hall to DeKoven Street in the heart of the Irish ghetto.

The street riots wore down the Know-Nothings, and they were thrown out of office the following year. The antibeer laws were repealed, and the Irish and Germans went back to fighting each other and drinking on Sundays. The Know-Nothing movement merged quietly into the strands of the new Republican party. The beer drinkers didn't forget that.

The years before the Civil War saw the formation of the Irish presence in the Democratic party. The Irish weren't having any of this business of government by the better elements; they were beginning to make their opinions loud and clear. When they had gathered enough strength and self-confidence, they would take it one step further and form the thing that came to be known as the Chicago Machine.

The Irish dominated early Chicago in a way they would not dominate Boston for another fifty years. They were a frightening presence to the few natives in the booming city that was doubling its population every few years.

The Irish were described by contemporaries in amazed tones. They were ambitious and rambunctious. The leading anti-Irish paper of the day, the *Chicago Tribune*, said in 1874: "Why are the instigators and ring leaders of our riots and tumults, in nine cases out of ten, Irishmen?"[2]

Again, in 1868, the *Tribune* sniffily described a Democratic party picnic held in the town of Lakeview (later part of the North Side of Chicago): "The majority of Irish present, true to the instincts of the lower orders of these people, had filled themselves early in the day with bad whiskey."[3]

The first Irishmen had arrived in 1838, the flood of Irish started in 1847, and by 1850 they made up 20 percent of the Chicago population. They lived all crowded together in their frame shanties west and south of the Loop and outraged the prairie sensibilities of Chicago's natives, but that did not dampen their enthusiasm for politics. In 1853, they held a quarter of all the public and political jobs in Chicago, an astounding achievement for a newly arrived immigrant group. They also filled up the ranks of the quasi-political jobs. They made up a third of the Chicago police force by 1865. They were a stunning presence in city government long before they gained real power and the top positions.

The remarkable rise to political prominence of the Chicago Irish was an accident of time and place. Chicago was unformed—the Irish could form it. Unlike the Germans and Swedes who arrived in great numbers at the same time, the Irish spoke the native language. Unlike the Germans and the Swedes, they broke out of their ghettoes early and moved all around the city, spreading the sense that they were omnipresent. They surprised apprehensive native Chicagoans with their social ease and enterprise.

The Irish idea of law and power became impossible to ignore in Chicago. They came from a country that had been run as an English colony, where justice was only for the few. The Irishman survived in his native land by guile and wit. It was better to get on the good side of a bad judge in County Clare than to depend on such English inventions as evidence and the rule of law.

By the time the Irish got there, Chicago was already operating its own simple political arrangement: there are no rules. The Irish formed this modus operandi into a code as rigid as Napoleon's. In Chicago it was always to be less important what you knew than who. Everything was for sale—and everyone. A wink and a nod was better than a man's word.

Wealth was power in Chicago only if you knew how to use power like a club. The city had been founded as a trading post, and the ethics of the frontier trader prevailed as the railroads brought in more trade. The flat prairie stretching out to infinity fed the fever for real estate speculation—and so did the railroad companies, which were mostly in the real estate business anyway. The greed for land—for the power of land and what it could do—became part of the political blood of the city as well.

2
Ragtime

THE CITY SPARKLED ON THE LAKE AND LOOKED TO BE THE coming greatest city on earth. New York was in its dotage, everyone agreed. Chicago was the new master of the continent, and it amazed itself. Population kept doubling, and the city flooded out across the prairie block by block and subsection by subsection, absorbing people faster than it could build housing for them. There was a constant hubbub of horses, voices, hammering, music and whorehouse laughter. St. Louis blues came north by train, and so did the odd black rhythm called ragtime. The city picked up the odd beat and mixed it with the Irish jig and German and Polish polkas and made music all night long.

The El was built around the loop of ground-level railroad tracks that ringed downtown, and it was a wonder of the time, snaking into the neighborhoods and connecting the separate cities contained in the one great city.

The great Palmer House Hotel was raised by screws out of the mud and built on a higher foundation. The whole city was lifted onto raised streets and sidewalks, built over vaulted concrete, so that the swamp was gradually filled in.

Landfill was dumped into the lake, making it smaller and the city bigger. Michigan Avenue, once on the shoreline, today lies nearly a mile to the west of the lake. After the great fire of 1871, the city built brick fireproof buildings and got a permanent look to itself. The first skyscrapers went up in Chicago, and architects heeded planner Daniel Burnham's advice to "make no little plans." Boulevards and parks were laid out. Chicago boasted on its city seal that it was *"Urbs in Horto"*—city in a garden, which sounded very fine to the citizens. Chicago would be greater than Paris, bigger than New York, more cultural than London. Oh, yes.

It was a wonderful, anything-goes city, unencumbered by a past, free of rigid castes and classes, still unformed and growing like a baby who does not know his strength. It was a bragging, mean, slaughtering, sweet-smelling, noisy carnival of a city with strong men and bearded ladies and a cast of koochy-koochy dancers especially laid on for the rubes flocking in from the prairie to see the latest in urban wickedness.

The growth was too fast for politics. While Tammany Hall was consolidating power in New York and machines were running in place in cities like Boston, Chicago politics was still stuck in the neighborhoods, in corner saloons and district whorehouses. In spite of their officeholders and policemen, the Irish couldn't put it together. The foot soldiers

were in place, but the leaders were still wrangling with each
other over who was going to call the shots once the Irish
takeover—which everyone understood was inevitable—finally occurred.

Twin impediments to control of Chicago by an Irish Machine were two men with one name—Carter Harrison and
his son. Father and son became mayor of Chicago five times
each between 1879 and 1915, the years that marked a kind of
zenith in Chicago not equalled until the Daley years.

Well educated and wealthy, the Harrisons were, as the
saying always goes in Chicago, personally honest. "Personally
honest" meant that they were never caught stealing, which
didn't mean that their friends didn't get their share of the
boodle. Sometimes the phrase is faintly damning—as when it
was applied to the ineffectual Mayor Martin Kennelly of the
early 1950s—or it can be meant as high praise and defense—
as when it described Richard J. Daley.

The Harrisons lived on Ashland Avenue on the West Side,
and some outsiders thought their contribution to local politics was a matter of noblesse oblige. Both men, in fact, were
skillful politicians who played the game—hard ball—for its
own sake. Though they dined with the best people, they were
equally comfortable with companions lower on the social
scale. Their tolerance reflected the strange tolerance of a city
that put the pragmatic ethics of the marketplace ahead of
any need to express the ethnic, religious and racial hatreds
they assuredly held. Chicago exuded a very practical sense of
laissez-faire.

Both Harrisons in their time made allies of the city's
saloonkeepers, gamblers and whorehouse keepers. Vice was
never unspeakable in Chicago as long as it turned a profit,
but it was generally thought advisable that it be contained in
certain neighborhoods so that it did not infect the whole city.

The lords of vice and the Harrisons concurred in this. In time, most of the city's vice came down to the sprawling Levee district on the South Side where every shocking act on earth was a nightly occurrence.

The parade of reformers who arrived in the city periodically at Union Station and prayed over Chicago defined what vice was: booze, first of all; then gambling; and then sex, in all its forms.

The primacy of liquor on the list was what confused the whole vice issue in Chicago, however. The popular evangelists of the time might thunder against the wicked habits of beer-swilling urban degenerates out on the prairies, but when they brought their troops into Chicago they found themselves greeted as often as not with derision. Liquor to Chicago's immigrant working population was a hard-earned glass in a neighborhood tavern with your pals, not demon rum dragging innocent farmers to perdition. After the major Lager Beer Riot of 1855, other riots stormed over the city whenever an unobservant city administration let a sneaky reformer pass a Sunday closing law or a new whiskey tax.

Both Harrisons understood this and allied themselves with the elements of tolerance. On election days when the power of the Harrisons was challenged, the saloonkeeper-politicians were torn between their ethnic political loyalties and the proven fact that the Harrisons knew just how to run a wide-open town. Economic self-interest won. The votes that were bought, stolen, or dug up in graveyards went to the Harrisons, time after time.

The Harrisons had no greater friends than the two aldermen from the vice-ridden First Ward that included the Loop and the Levee. The short one was John Kenna, called Hinky Dink. He had the face of an Irish undertaker, a little twitching mustache and the most notorious political saloon in the

city, the Workingmen's Exchange on Van Buren Street at the
south end of the Loop.

His partner in graft, corruption and vice was a fellow with
a big barrel of a belly who wore emerald green suits of his
own design. Bathhouse John Coughlin moved about like a
three-dimensional map of Ireland. He was given to reciting
bad doggerel verse, mostly written by himself.

Carter Harrison II came to call the honorable aldermen
from the First Ward his "Rocks of Gibraltar." It was their
vote-buying and solidly crooked electioneering that returned
him to office again and again. For their part, the sentimental
rogues called him "Our Carter"—and he certainly was. When
Hinky Dink finally went off to the Great Election Judge in
the Sky in the 1940s, police broke open his safety deposit box
and found within, among the bonds, a collection of Christmas cards he had received over the years from his pal Carter.
But if there was a thread of real affection in their relationship, it did not interfere with the business of politics.

Hinky Dink and the Bathhouse shared the graft of their
ward and were the political protectors of the vice that generated it. Among those protected were the Everleigh sisters,
Ada and Minna, two prim Southern dowagers who ran the
most elite whorehouse in America. It was said that only the
richest railroad magnates, businessmen and politicians were
permitted to lay their bodily parts on the girls kept by the
sisters. The whole of Chicago society whispered about the
house kept by the Everleighs, and they were an uplifting
inspiration to lesser whoremasters.

Lest the romance of the time sweep you up, there were
meaner elements on the Levee, like the whorehouses popu-
lated by dazed farmgirls kidnapped off the prairies by gangs
who specialized in such trafficking. They were doped, abused,
used and abandoned, and sometimes they were simply killed

because they were not useful any more. (The Mann Act against what was called "white slavery" was introduced by a Chicago congressman to stop abduction-for-sex centered in wicked Chicago in the 1920s.)

If you couldn't get it in Chicago, you couldn't get it. There were permanent floating crap games and permanent fixed games; there were dope dens (largely for Orientals in the burgeoning Chinatown at the south end of the Levee district, and for blacks); bars and flophouses for the itinerant gandy dancers and drifters.

The rule of non-law was fixed, particularly on election days. The saloonkeeper-politicians strutted their stuff in all the city neighborhoods that day, but nowhere more grandly than in the First Ward.

A *Chicago Daily News* reporter named Ben Hecht tried to give some idea of what a Chicago Election Day was like in the era of ragtime: "The voting centers we reporters covered were usually in cigar stores, saloon back rooms, or commandeered Chinese laundries.

"There were as yet no voting machines. The voter stepped gingerly into a curtained-off space, sat down at a rickety table, and with heart in mouth, marked his vote on the ballot with a pencil. His heart was in his mouth because there was always a likelihood that a hefty 'election watcher' might dart in and catch him voting for the wrong side.

"The election watchers were put in the field by both political parties. Their duty was to make sure the voter was not unduly influenced in marking his ballot."

How influenced? Why, with free liquor, a free flop, a free lunch in the saloon, a patronage appointment or, when flattery failed, the promise, said Hecht, "of assault and battery. Most of the election judges were ruffians wearing badges."

Votes were also stolen by "short pencil men" who palmed

pencil stubs as they counted ballots so they could add marks to an opposition vote ballot and render it invalid. Of course, the stuffing of ballot boxes prevailed as the accepted method of ensuring a correct vote. "A day or two before the election," wrote Hecht, "the vital wards of the town filled up with hordes of drunks, hopheads, and bearded hoboes."

Hinky Dink and Bathhouse John worked out of their huge Workingmen's Exchange saloon to do the right thing for their friends, particularly the Harrisons. "A few days before the election, the shabby hotels of the First Ward would start swarming with new guests. The arrivals, minus suitcases and often last names, were jammed six to a small room. They slept on a cold floor, with burlap bags as covering. But day-time was a fete. Free liquor, free hops, free prostitutes were theirs for the asking. Come election day, the grateful floaters voted four or five times in different precincts. They gave different names, but the suspicious opposition could check and find all the aliases in the flophouse registries. The morn-ing after election, they came shuffling or reeling into The Workingmen's Exchange to receive a final bonus for their democratic activities. The bonus ran from two to five dollars, depending on the amount of voting done."[1]

Voting excesses were not unique to Chicago—but they were on a large scale, and Hecht was only one of many observers who remarked on the tolerance and even admiration with which the ordinary Chicagoan regarded them.

The memory of the ragtime years was still strong in the 1930s when Prohibition was repealed. Among the rules writ-ten into the city's new liquor law were prohibitions against the free lunch in any place that sold alcohol and injunctions against calling a saloon a saloon. Until the 1970s, saloons could not be open on election days.

At the beginning of the century, the city had an amazing

one hundred aldermen representing fifty wards. The un-
wieldy body of the Chicago City Council offered a vision of
political fragmentation and a patchwork of competing
fiefdoms. Political corruption was wide open in nineteenth-
century Chicago, and it merely changed its form as the twentieth century took shape.

Lincoln Steffens, a reporter for *McClure's Magazine*, wrote
a series of articles on urban corruption collected as *The Shame
of the Cities*. Steffens called the aldermen on the Chicago City
Council "the gray wolves" for the color of their hair and the
rapacious cunning and greed of their natures. He described
the systematized graft in the city as "boodling."

An example of what Steffens was talking about is the story
of Charles Yerkes, a businessman who sought a city franchise
in the same way that many others had in a smaller way.
Yerkes wanted control over the city right-of-way for his trac-
tion (streetcar) company. He simply bribed enough aldermen with enough money so that they voted him the
monopoly. It was quite open, even bragged about. To a Chicago alderman, the only thing in the deal to be ashamed of
would have been getting less out of it than you could have.

Little changed in the next eighty years. Corruption of aldermen with bribes for city contracts has continued at an
unflagging pace (though the number of aldermen, in the
interest of economy, has been reduced to fifty). Alderman
Thomas Keane, Mayor Daley's City Council leader, spent a
couple of years in federal prison on a mail fraud conviction
in a real estate deal. (Released from prison, he went to work
for Mayor Jane Byrne, drawing up a gerrymandered reap-
portionment map for the City Council that preserved a white
majority. It was later thrown out by a federal court, and
Mayor Byrne explained that she employed Keane because of
his brains and his experience in government.)

Eighty years after Lincoln Steffens talked about "gray wolves," Alderman Edward Burke resurrected the term to proudly—and accurately—describe his colleagues. The venality of city aldermen continued to be legendary, but as long as they satisfied the neighborhoods, their reputation didn't matter. Let them sell the streets—but pick up the garbage on time in the ward.

In the "reform" regime of Mayor Harold Washington a vast federal investigation found some of his supporters supping at the table of a bribe-giving company intent on getting a contract to dispose of city waste. What goes around comes around in Chicago, and politics is still about money and garbage.

The excuses for taking the money so routinely offered by bribe-givers continue to be imaginative. Alderman Perry Hutchinson, a supporter of Mayor Washington in the City Council, explained in 1986 that he *did* take money from FBI mole Anthony Raymond who was trying to see if members of the Council were corrupt—but he was using the money to help the poor in his ward.

At least there was gaiety in the days of the old First Ward of Hinky Dink and Bathhouse John. Once a year the aldermen of the First Ward threw a very public party for the more adventurous elements of Chicago society. This annual ball was held in the old Coliseum on South Wabash. The Coliseum had started out as a Confederate prison and had been transported to Chicago, stone by stone, and reconstructed as an exhibition hall.

At the appointed hour, drays and coaches pulled up to the main entrance, disgorging pimps, whores, murderers, molesters, gangsters and gunmen and gandy dancers from the railroad yards. Just about every reporter in town came down to join in the fun. The Everleigh sisters graciously welcomed the guests, and a grand march was held as the finale. In between, there was good liquor, hot dancing and the occasional shooting. Hinky Dink decreed that no one was supposed to bring a gun or knife with him in his formal wear, but boys will be boys, and a fellow had to protect himself. Sometimes, in the excitement of the occasion, a participant forgot his manners.

Why did the city tolerate this? It perplexed Ben Hecht: "The good people who read newspapers and worked honestly for a living and raised decent families and profited not a penny from political skulduggeries—these pious and honorable folk were thrilled always to read our exposés of the town's villains. They were also fascinated by the same rogues and at election time seemed to prefer them to honest office seekers."[2]

He offered a theory about why this should be so: "The good-citizen majority looked on the wrongdoers as a sort of vaudeville, more entertaining than harmful. They watched these vaudevillians bilk the town, batten on its vices, and their virtuous citizen hearts applauded furtively. The parlors and bedrooms in which honest folk lived were (as now) rather dull places. It was pleasant, in a way, to know that outside their windows, the devil was still capering in a flare of brimstone."[3]

THE HARRISONS AND THEIR LIEUTENANTS STAYED IN POWER BEcause they made it a point to support Irish causes. Even Irish in the second, third, fourth and fifth generations identified strongly with the mother country to an extraordinary—and belligerent—degree. It was this lingering, intense clannishness and warlike posture, seeing a slight at every turn, that made the Irish so formidable in politics, even when Germans and, later, Poles had greater numbers in the city.

Because he understood this, Harrison Senior continued as mayor—he was acceptable enough to the lower ranks of Irish politicos, who continued to quarrel among themselves and failed to come up with alternative leadership.

In 1895, a disgruntled office seeker named Eugene Prendergast put the question of Irish political leadership on the front burner by strolling to the Harrison manse on Ashland Avenue and shooting Carter *père* dead.

A little-known Irishman named John P. Hopkins succeeded as mayor and filled out the remaining two years of Harrison's term. But he had too many enemies among too many factions in the Irish tribe and not enough friends.

Hopkins was a belligerent Irishman. When he heard that a political critic named Graham Harris had predicted that Carter Harrison Junior would beat him in the coming election, he went to the man to ask if it was true. It was indeed, said Mr. Harris. Hopkins popped him in the nose and told the *Chicago Tribune* later: "I'll give him number 2 as soon as I see him again."[4]

Alas for Hopkins, Harris was right. The Irish dithering continued, and Hopkins was knocked out in the 1898 primary by young Carter Harrison, who succeeded to the old family job. His reign of genial corruption—the salad days of the old gray wolves—continued until 1915.

THE CHARACTER OF CHICAGO WAS SET BETWEEN 1890 AND 1915. As the Irish say, the city was full of itself; it looked in the mirror in the morning and liked what it saw. You couldn't say a word agin' it.

It is true that some cities have a female character and some are male. Chicago's masculinity was exactly captured by Carl

Sandburg in his poem. It was the "stormy, husky, brawling/ City of the Big Shoulders."

The crowning moment of this era was the 1893 Columbian Exposition, marking Columbus' discovery of the New World 401 years earlier. The fair was sanctioned by an international committee in Paris and was snatched by Chicago from New York. It opened a year late and was magnificent—even the snobbish Henry Adams admitted being struck with awe when he visited the fairgrounds on the south lakefront.

The fair confirmed the magnificence of the city itself. Chicago sprang up on the barren prairie by magic—perhaps it was Oz itself, as conceived by one of its natives, L. Frank Baum, who wrote his books while working as a copywriter in Chicago.

The city had a million people now and was still doubling in size every few years. It grew through annexation because it had what the surrounding towns needed—a steady water supply and a good sewer system. The water came from far out in clear Lake Michigan and the flow of the Chicago River into the lake was reversed in a gigantically complex feat of engineering so that the river could be Chicago's prime sewer. It still is.

One of the towns annexed early in the 1890s was Hyde Park, where the University of Chicago was born in 1891. Financed heavily by Rockefeller millions, the Gothic-designed university has grown into one of the great schools of the world.

Chicago was learning that culture wasn't the worst thing in the world. Jenny Lind sang in Chicago and said she liked the town, and when Oscar Wilde came through and insulted the looks of the old Water Tower—well, it was the price you paid for culture. Every European visitor who recorded his impressions of Chicago at the time felt it necessary to emphasize how vital and vulgar the place was.

For a brief time the city was the center of the fledgling movie industry—until some genius discovered that the sun always shone in California.

By 1910, jazz had traveled north from New Orleans on the Illinois Central line. Black-and-tan clubs abounded in the whorehouse district of the Levee and the music played was pure soul. The Black Belt—a rigidly segregated housing district that ran south of the Levee—started growing in the years just before World War I.

The parts commingled, the elegant city running stride by stride with the vulgar. The magnificent buildings of the Columbian Exposition inspired the architecture of the next thirty years—and the dance style of Little Egypt doing the koochy-koo on the bawdy Midway at the fair became the rage for Chicagoans.

The cynical, knowing and deeply sarcastic dialogue of the average Chicagoan was formed in these years, similar in wit and tone to the speech of Berliners. For example, if you carried a fat gut bespeaking gluttony, it was called an "alderman." Chicagoans said they had the finest police force that money could buy.

Reformers were attracted to Chicago because it was so blatant about its corruption. The reputation of the city still is largely due to its public honesty about its public corruption. Other cities have crooked cops, crooked politicians, crooked judges and crooked political organizations—but they are not celebrated. Mike Royko's mocking chronicles of municipal chicanery echo ragtime's sly saloonkeeper-commentator, Mr. Dooley (created by Finley Peter Dunne). As Mr. Dooley once observed about the roughhouse nature of local politics: "It ain't bean-bag."[5]

If the city's character was formed in those twenty-five years, so was the character of the last great political Machine. While the free-wheeling days of Hinky Dink, Bathhouse John, "Our Carter," Yerkes and other villains of note continued, within the Democratic party the foundations of an Irish political machine were being laid down. Ironically, the builder of this Machine would not live to see its triumph and, just as ironically, it would take a tough Bohemian coal miner to fuse the Irish parts into a single working organism of political power.

3

The Gas Man

WILLIAM JENNINGS BRYAN AND ROGER SULLIVAN WERE BORN in rural Illinois towns, separated only by a few months and a couple of hundred miles of farm land. Bryan went on to become the embodiment of rural American virtue, the great orator who took the Democratic party over with his impassioned injunction not to crucify man on a cross of gold. Sullivan took a different path and ended up as the arch rival of Bryan and his breed in politics: the slick city pol, the backroom dealer, the Machine man moved only to faint contempt by all oratory and all orators.

Sullivan left rural Belvidere at the age of nineteen in 1879 and headed for Chicago, some eighty miles away. He worked in a West Side railway yard for $1.25 a day. Sullivan had brains and ambition, and he began to get into politics in a small way. A few years later he was known as a ward boss; but being a ward boss in those days meant being one of a few dozen independent operators. Sullivan, however, found the game congenial, and he had ideas. He was no backslapping saloon politician. He was always to be described as quiet, calculating, affable, not a good hater but never a man who ran from a fight. In these years he made alliances, particularly with John Hopkins, another businessman-politician who was ahead of his time.

Their enemy, as they saw it, was genial Carter Harrison and the whole saloonkeeper crowd that held power in the neighborhoods, and particularly in the Levee district of the First Ward. Power through the saloons was denied Hopkins and Sullivan, so they turned to business.

By the accident of Prendergast assassinating Carter Harrison in 1895, Hopkins became mayor. His good friend Sullivan then put together something called the Ogden Gas Company, a "company" on paper only. Another pal, Martin B. Madden, a Republican alderman, introduced an ordinance in City Council enfranchising the company to do business in the city.

This bit of sleight-of-hand was so common, there was a name for it: it was called a mace. Sullivan's mace was intended to bludgeon wealthy Peoples Gas into buying up the Ogden Gas Company at an inflated price in order to hold on to its monopoly in the city.

Mayor Hopkins approved the Madden ordinance and Sullivan waited on Peoples Gas; but when the gas company refused to be conned, Ogden Gas went operational. Sullivan undercut the price of gas to force Peoples to play with him: Peoples charged two dollars a thousand-foot for gas. Ogden charged ninety cents. Everyone knew that Sullivan was working a con, that he could not afford to charge only ninety cents, but there seemed no way to stop him.

While this business blackmail was continuing, Sullivan was defining his ideas of a disciplined political machine in which jobs and favors were awarded on a scale model of the Tammany Hall system. Unlike Tammany, the Sullivan machine did not have all the horses. The Irish were still divided into the faction favoring Sullivan-Hopkins and the one for Carter Harrison II, who would oppose Hopkins in the race for mayor.

By contemporary accounts, Sullivan was the model of a modern Machine boss. He kept track of who owed what to whom, but he did it without malice or emotion. A genial man with a soft voice and a persuasive manner, he worked to include more people in his organization rather than to exclude them. Harrison earned his enmity by scornfully calling Sullivan "the gas man," a nickname that stuck (and which, in later years, Sullivan grew fond of).

The gas game grew serious when the city decided to legislate the maximum price of gas at eighty-five cents. This meant the Ogden company would have to drop its price by five cents—but Peoples would have to cut its price by more than half. Peoples threw up its hands and surrendered and agreed to merge Ogden Gas into the larger utility. Roger Sullivan became a millionaire with that deal and retired from the gas business.

He was, however, a partner with Hopkins in a dredging firm called Great Lakes Dock and Dredging that got a lot of city business. In weekly sessions at the round table in the Sherman House Hotel, Sullivan and Hopkins explained to their followers the principles of these and other arrangements; the principles, in fact, of the new politician.

The old politician, an independent operator, was content to knock down a little graft to allow businessmen to make monopolies and fortunes. The new Machine politician, using the disciplined approach to government, became both politician and businessman. He was the city and he did business with the city.

Thus, disciples like George Brennan and the Bohemian Jewish leader Adolph Sabath discovered the wealth to be made by providing bonding for enterprises approved by the city. Construction companies bought into by Sullivanites suddenly did very well on lucrative city contracts. Fortunes were made in insurance businesses and firms that provided transportation for the city, as well as school lunches and textbooks and office supplies—all in a growing and interconnected "organization of friends and neighbors."

Though Sullivan's Machine and the ways it became wealthy seem primitive to today's student of political science, it was innovative in its day because it applied the principle of investment for maximum future profits to a disciplined political organization.

One of the brightest of the Sullivan disciples at the Sherman House Hotel round table was George Brennan, a well-spoken and cultivated man whose conversation was turned with self-mocking humor. He had lost his right leg in a childhood accident and his great, hulking, limping figure was a theatrical presence in the various halls of Chicago government. A schoolteacher in his youth, Brennan even served as state secretary of education briefly during the troubled regime of Governor John Peter Altgeld. (Altgeld sacrificed his career in politics when he pardoned four anarchists condemned to death for their part in the 1886 Haymarket Riot in Chicago.)

Brennan had contempt for excesses of any kind. He believed that a disciplined machine functioned well and quietly.

He had no illusions about himself or his associates. He once turned to writer Frank R. Kent at some political event or other and asked: "Why do you suppose they let us run it?"[1]

He meant the people. He was constantly surprised at their tolerance of corruption.

In time, he learned the Sullivan game very well and became an underwriter of bonds. In one three-year period at the Sanitary District in Chicago, where he wrote bonds on contractors, he collected $625,750 for a few strokes of the pen.

Brennan was a man of a deep cynicism that worked well in Illinois politics. During the First World War, he pushed the legislature to pass as an economy measure a "non-merit selection" bill for the state judiciary. Instead of going through the tedious process of selecting qualified jurists from the ranks of lawyers by a merit committee, future candidates for the state courts would be chosen by the political parties and put to a democratic vote.

This system is still in force in Illinois though it is routinely decried by editorialists and lawyers' associations as ensuring overrepresentation of mediocrity on the bench. The point was brought home forcefully in Chicago in the 1980s with the indictment and conviction of four Cook County judges who routinely took bribes from lawyers who had cases pending in their courts. The judicial defense in these cases was that the bribes were really unsecured loans. The defense did not hold and the judges went to jail.

The Brennan judicial "reform" added another strong support to the building of the Machine. In time, the Machine would control the judicial process, the legislative process and the administrative process in Chicago and in the state capital.

Roger Sullivan and George Brennan and their friends were not the first to see the possibilities in linking city contracts and private businesses controlled by political officials. But the scale and efficiency with which they worked was unprecedented. Sullivan contended that the boodle was a crude, one-shot way of amassing money. Be quiet, efficient and consistent, he argued, and the rewards would be so much greater.

Though Sullivan was, obviously, not an idealist, he has been credited with sending an arch idealist to the White House. In 1912, at the Democratic National Convention in Baltimore, Champ Clark of Missouri held the majority vote but could not push it over the required two thirds. Sullivan's son, a student at Princeton, urged his father to throw the Illinois delegation for Wilson because he was "a great man." Sullivan had little interest in the matter—Washington could do nothing for Chicago—but his son's sudden interest in politics intrigued him.

In any case, whoever became the Democratic nominee, it was unlikely he would win. Democrats did not win the presidency.

At a dramatic point in the voting, Sullivan is reported to have crossed the aisle to speak with the New York delegate Charles Murphy of Tammany. He told Murphy the time had come to start delivering the votes to Wilson to break the deadlock. Murphy said he would think it over.

Sullivan went back, sat down, and when "Illinois" was called from the speaker's rostrum, the delegation flipped to Wilson and the rush was on. Tammany and New York went to Wilson on the same vote and Wilson won the nomination. In the strange general election that followed—the Republicans split in two and William Howard Taft was pitted against the Bull Moose candidacy of Theodore Roosevelt—Wilson won narrowly. Being a good idealist, he promptly announced his door was closed to political bosses like Roger Sullivan.

Sullivan worked very hard to discipline a state party that

rarely won state elections. He established the Machine principle of controlling the primary at all costs. Whoever the Machine selected as candidate was the candidate who would win the primary. This elementary rule was at the core of the Machine—it might lose general elections but it never lost a primary. It was that principle that was challenged by Jane Byrne in 1979, and when she beat the Machine mayoral candidate, Mike Bilandic, the Machine started to fall apart.

Sullivan's great enemy in the national party was the vitriolic old fundamentalist, William Jennings Bryan. He lashed at Sullivan at every opportunity, and because he had a strong following in southern Illinois, tried to do Sullivan damage on his own turf. He called the Sullivan crowd "road agents" and "porch climbers," which played well in Peoria. Despite this, Sullivan nominated himself for U.S. senator in 1914, following the national prominence gained in electing Wilson, and he ran true to form—he won the primary and lost the election.

By 1915, another Chicago mayoralty election was at hand, and this time, despite his ups and downs, Roger Sullivan had just about built the Machine he wanted. It was frankly modeled on the organization of Tammany Hall but with Chicago touches. Sullivan's lieutenant, George Brennan, was to "depersonalize" the Machine—to run it through a central county committee—so that no one faction would be identified with the running of it. There was plenty for all. At Sullivan's direction, the Cook County Democratic central committee voted itself complete control of all Democratic patronage. To make certain that control meant control, all Democratic officeholders were ordered to send the names of each man on their payrolls to the committee. No officeholder was ever again to consider any job seeker unless he had a letter from his ward or township committeeman stating that he was approved for the job. This was the signal and famous institution of the "committeeman's letter" that anti-Machine reformers were still promising to eliminate seventy years later and that the Machine was still saying did not exist except as a figment of a newspaper's imagination. To understand the brutal simplicity of this patronage system is to understand the title of the late Milton Rakove's 1975 study of the Machine and its culture: *We Don't Want Nobody Nobody Sent.*[2]

Sullivan intended to use the Machine in 1915 to control the mayor's office and even to make himself the Democratic vice-presidential candidate in 1916. But his Machine—still in its infancy—was suddenly thrown off the tracks by a crooked buffoon with a clown's face and the mind of a demagogue.

4

The Demagogue of Prairie Avenue

WILLIAM HALE THOMPSON WAS TO THE PRAIRIE AVENUE mansion born. Today, the mansions of South Prairie Avenue are undergoing pathetic and partial restoration and there is even a Prairie Avenue Historic District that sits in isolation hemmed in by a network of expressway overpasses, derelict factory buildings and printing companies and railroad yards. In that little stretch of Prairie Avenue at 18th Street, you can still get some sense of what it must have been like to be part of the "Prairie Avenue crowd."

The rich were not quiet about it in an earlier day. The Potter Palmers and Marshall Fields and their kind built mansions of Illinois limestone and fieldstone to proclaim to people outside the kind of people who lived inside. The elegant city was beginning to distance itself from the neighborhoods.

William Hale Thompson, "Big Bill" as he came to be called, grew up in this neighborhood, but that doesn't explain him. Explaining Thompson is like explaining earthquakes. There is some reason that they occur, but it's too complicated to go into and the disaster is still the same.

Like Jane Byrne sixty-five years later, Big Bill was a political wild card, thrown into the hand at the last moment and completely changing the game. Thompson beat the Machine in its fragile infancy in 1915; Jane Byrne beat it in 1979 when it was an empty shell waiting to be cracked.

Both were probably the best campaigners in the history of the city. They were absolutely ruthless in attack (a much-admired quality in Chicago), and they were willing to sink to any level of mudslinging on a whim. They were immensely entertaining while tearing the town apart.

Other similarities come to mind: both attracted the neglected black vote and made it work to win office. Both favored policies supported by the criminal element—a wide-open city with lots of vice (Byrne's support of legal casino gambling even appalled her police chief). Both came from well-off families with good addresses behind them.

Thompson loved politics from an early age, and by class and inclination, he was a Republican. He was elected alderman from the Second Ward—his home, South Side territory—with the support of the wealthy and the blacks who were constrained in the Black Belt just south of the Levee and just west of where Thompson lived. Thompson was colorblind and black people saw that as a good thing.

What Thompson loved was campaigning. He served only one term in the City Council. The business of government bored him and he did not distinguish himself, but it is hard to be colorful when your seatmates include Hinky Dink and Bathhouse John.

He ran next for the county board, won the seat and was bored again. By 1915, teamed up with his mentor Fred Lundin (called "the poor Swede" because he was not poor at all, having made a fortune selling a drink called Juniper Ade on street corners), he ran for the Republican nomination for mayor. His primary opponent was Judge Harry Olson, and Thompson's campaign against Olson was a dandy. Thompson supporters put out an anonymous pamphlet in which it was charged that Judge Olson's wife was a Catholic and that because of this disgraceful situation, Olson would "deliberately destroy the public school system" in Chicago.

Thompson was not anti-Catholic, mind; he was hardly against anything. He just did what he had to do to win, and most of the Catholics were busy in the Democratic side of the primary, deciding on Roger Sullivan's handpicked candidate for mayor, Robert Sweitzer.

Sullivan saw victory clearly ahead. Controlling the mayor's job would mean controlling thousands of city payroll jobs and would give the Machine the clout necessary to fix itself permanently into the fabric of Chicago government.

Sullivan crushed the weakened Carter Harrison faction in the primary, and his men and his Machine turned then to crush the cowboy from Prairie Avenue who wore ten gallon hats and snorted whiskey until his face was as bloated as ten pounds of unbaked dough.

Thompson floored Sullivan and the Machine with an ingenious bag of tricks. The war in Europe was only a year old and the United States was still two years shy of getting in it. Stories of alleged German atrocities were already forming public opinion against the Kaiser in America—but not in singular, isolated Chicago.

Thompson decided to run against the King of England. He ran from neighborhood to neighborhood, mounting platforms on streetcorners, in town halls and in saloons, and he denounced the bloody British for making war upon the Fatherland. The Chicago Germans loved it. Sympathy for Thompson swelled along Lincoln Avenue that cuts diagonally through "Germantown" on the Northwest Side.

His opponent was caught napping. Sweitzer had not thought to develop a foreign policy plank in his bid for mayor of Chicago. As he struggled to regain momentum, Thompson was charging on with the subtlety of Patton's Third Army.

Thompson invaded the Irish precincts—the base of the Sullivan Machine—and he kept up the fight with the lifeless British punching bag he used in German neighborhoods. The Irish were speechless and mesmerized into quiescence by this foul-mouthed giant who seemed ready to invade Cornwall with a contingent of boys from Bridgeport.

His anti-Catholic stance in the Republican primary, used to effect against Olson, was forgotten by the Irish in the general election because Thompson's hatred for the British got the better of them. Incredibly, while keeping up his dukes in the Irish wards, Thompson also courted the Protestant Swedes on the North Side by insisting that a Sweitzer victory would mean a Catholic cabal controlling the public school board. He was all things to all men and it all worked.

Thompson cut a gallant figure as he invaded Irish churches and preached that the thirty-two counties of Ireland deserved Home Rule and that he, Thompson, was the dearest friend of Ireland that the Irish could ever hope to find.

Sweitzer tried to find his own level in the Thompson mudpit. His stunned managers put together a "Dear Fatherland" letter translated into German, Austrian and Hungarian and distributed it in the appropriate neighborhoods in

Chicago. The letter pointed out that Sweitzer—note the name—was a dear friend of the German Empire and always had been. "Stand shoulder to shoulder in this election," the letter urged. "As our countrymen in the trenches and on the high seas are fighting for the preservation of our dear fatherland. The election of a German-American would be a fitting answer to the defamers of the fatherland. . . ."[1]

The letter backfired.

It upset a number of prominent German-American leaders who wished to remain neutral in the European struggle, perhaps foreseeing American involvement and the draconian anti-German measures pushed through by the Wilson Administration during and after the war. They accused Sweitzer of ethnic baiting and gave Thompson a pass, largely because Thompson had been wise enough not to put anything down on paper.

The letter backfired a second time when Thompson's manager, Fred Lundin, made sure it was translated into Polish and distributed to the thousands and thousands of Polish voters in the city whose homeland had been swallowed up by Russia and Germany and who now saw the war as a chance to get their country back. The Poles counted in Chicago, where more of them were to settle than in any other city in the world outside of Warsaw.

No vote was ignored, not even the black vote, which was conceded ahead of time to the Republicans by the Irish Machine of Roger Sullivan. Thompson went after it. He had a strange rapport with blacks in Chicago, perhaps because he talked to them in a straightforward way, not as backward children. He promised protection from police harassment for their gambling enterprises and he promised them jobs.

Charles Merriam, a thoughtful University of Chicago professor from Hyde Park who had run as the Sullivan faction's candidate for mayor in 1911 and lost, explained Thompson's hold on blacks: "To be recognized and represented by a crook is better than not to be recognized or represented at all."[2]

Thompson's ally in courting black support in this and future elections was George F. Harding, another member of the Prairie Avenue crowd. Harding was a wealthy insurance executive and his insurance policies—called burial policies—were in black hands throughout the Black Belt. He made his money dime by dime, from the weekly payments of poor blacks who feared their deaths would lead to paupers' graves. Harding also had vast real estate holdings in the black Second Ward and he knew how to get the Thompson message out to his tenants in his slums.

THOMPSON WAS SHAMELESS AND IN HIGH SPIRITS AS HE DUMPED all over Sullivan and his carefully constructed Machine. He even appealed to non-voters—women—to urge their menfolk to help his cause. He said he was a reformer and that when he became mayor, he would put a woman on the school board. He said his election would be a message that "the crooks had better move out of town."[3] (In fact, his election was to lead to the permanent partnership of the crime syndicate and City Hall, but no one knew that yet.)

He used any weapon that worked, particularly anti-Catholicism. The Sullivan Machine was Irish and that meant Catholic and so, beat up the Catholics (though not when courting them). He titillated Protestant church ladies with stories of how the Sullivan Machine was controlled by the Pope.

Thompson won the election by tailoring each lie to suit the prejudices of his audience. The people of Chicago got the mayor they deserved because they wanted to believe the worst about everyone else.

5
Jazztime

BLUSTERING BIG BILL WAS MAYOR. HE HAD WHIPPED THE carefully constructed Machine of Roger Sullivan and George Brennan. It was 1915, two years before U.S. entry in the war, and America—and Chicago—glanced back at the end of an era.

Big Bill Thompson was bored as mayor almost immediately, but he was never bored with life. He dressed as outrageously as he talked, often showing up at civic functions wearing cowboy boots and a ten-gallon hat. He told people he dressed in this peculiar way because he lived "by the cowboy code." When he took vacations—which he did often enough—he went west, rode horses, packed six-guns. Yet no one in Chicago seemed embarrassed by him at first.

A restless mood of vague reform was building in the country, fanned by people like the high-minded Woodrow Wilson. Such people saw restraint of the liquor trade as a key to reform.

The winds of reform blew into the squat gray City Hall where Thompson reigned in a lackadaisical way. Thompson declared his sympathies for reform and announced that the moribund 1872 saloon-closing ordinance would now be enforced in Chicago. Riots were predicted, echoing the riots held the last time someone had tried to enforce the ordinance.

But nothing happened. Big Bill was as good as his word— which was worthless. What he said was not necessarily what he did. The saloons stayed open and the reformers went home and all seemed well . . . except that the threat implied by Thompson's words stirred up the saloonkeepers who had already formed the United Societies, an organization intended to fight any overt manifestation of the Prohibition fever sweeping the rest of the country.

The position of Chicago was perilous. Surrounded on all sides by God-fearing, rural, dry-as-dust hick towns where the word of the Lord was preached—though the part about drinking wine at Cana was glossed over—the City of Big Shoulders and strong thirst stomped out even mere words of antiliquor support with the fervor of a forest ranger stomping out a campfire in July. United Societies assembled a large group and marched on City Hall to state its position. The group was led by a small-time Bohemian politician from the West Side named Anton Cermak who had gradually made himself the spokesman for the liquor interests. It was an honorable position, it paid well, it elevated Tough Tony in the ranks of the wets, and besides, he could drink any ten men under the table.

That small confrontation in 1915 at City Hall would symbolize the coming confusion of reform and Prohibition. One became synonymous with the other. And the opposites would attract as well. Big Bill Thompson would placate his reformist critics from time to time by returning to his pose as champion of the "dry" movement in Chicago—all the while turning over the keys and locks of the city to the powerful Chicago underworld.

Thompson's administration was marked by corruption, graft and the usual selling of jobs and city services. The Thompson gang made a specialty of squeezing graft out of the city school system by arranging contracts with favored suppliers, selling insurance and taking over school board real estate and reselling it at a profit—a profit that went not to the school board, but into the pockets of Thompson cronies.

(In time, Thompson's mentor and spiritual godfather, Fred Lundin, was indicted for his part in the school board corruption. It happened while Big Bill was on vacation in Hawaii, but he rushed back to Chicago and got the finest attorney money could buy to defend his pal. Clarence Darrow, who once served as city corporation counsel under "our Carter," did his damnedest to get Fred off, and he succeeded. But then, as Darrow himself put it in the city he loved: "There is no justice—in or out of court.")

The spirit of reform found a real opportunity in 1917 when Woodrow Wilson, who ran in 1916 on a platform of keeping America out of the European war, flip-flopped in on the British side and sent our boys overseas. It was a move that worked out well for those who didn't die in the trenches. The war was brief, the American part in the victory was clear and Wilson captured a world stage. The virtue the country was feeling was the force needed to nail the Prohibition amendment onto the Constitution.

The city of innumerable beer riots, where grown men had risked life and limb to defend the right to drink in saloons, was chagrined. The temperance battallions had won, and booze was being poured down the drains.

But the chagrin was shortlived. At least some Chicagoans saw a new and even more profitable way to make money on the backs of reformers.

CHICAGO GOT THE LATTER-DAY IMMIGRANTS, BY AND LARGE, because the town was new and far beyond the pioneer settlements on the East Coast. This is why there are so many Eastern Europeans in the city compared with New York, Philadelphia and Boston; it also explains the large number of Sicilians.

The Sicilians brought to the New World their wit, their food, their industry and their Mafia. In the Italian ghettoes of the East (and, gradually, in the "little Italy" that burgeoned on the near West Side of Chicago in a neighborhood called Taylor Street and another at 24th and Oakley), the Black Hand societies ran those illegal activities that had their counterparts in the militant secret societies of the Irish. It was a link with the Old World and old ways and it was a bad one.

With the advent of Prohibition, the Italian and Irish criminal gangs of Chicago quickly set up in the liquor business, following the classic business principle—give the customer what he wants.

The Italian gangs came to dominate the city because they were simply better at the business of crime. The boss, Johnny Torrio, imported a Sicilian immigrant from New York to help him in the business. The bright young man found gold in Chicago streets. His name was Alphonse Capone, and he was very good at what he did.

Capone, like Sullivan and Brennan, was a planner and organizer. He organized distribution and production just like any good middle-management executive. Within five years of the enactment of the Eighteenth Amendment, there were fifteen breweries running full tilt inside the limits of the city and more than fifteen thousand retail outlets—more than there are today when liquor is legal again. Chicago cops were becoming rich with the bribes received for letting the speakeasies alone and federal authorities sent to Chicago to clean out the illegal trade estimated that Torrio and Capone were each taking in $100,000 a week in 1924 by satisfying the thirst in the dry Midwest.

Capone carefully built the first non-family-based syndicate of men devoted to like-minded goals. In his way, he was the Roger Sullivan of crime, systematizing that which had previously existed in chaos. He literally put part of the Chicago police department on his weekly payroll. He was ruthless with competition, whether it came from rival Italian gangs or Irish ones.

In 1924, methodically organizing the syndicate, Capone dispatched the Gemma brothers to the North Side florist shop of his rival, Dion O'Bannion. O'Bannion recognized the boys and stuck out his hand in greeting. One of them held the handshake so that O'Bannion was temporarily immobilized while the other blew the life out of him with a pistol. The passing of O'Bannion prompted retaliatory commando raids by the Irish remnants on the North Side and four of the Gemma brothers were killed in four months, but Capone was now king of beer. He became something of a local hero, quoted often in local and national publications. His politics were conservative; he believed in the sanctity of the family and in God.

CORRUPTION FLOURISHED UNDER THE BENIGN REIGN OF BIG Bill Thompson, the man who lived the cowboy code. For example, one Capone groupie was a *Chicago Tribune* reporter named Jake Lingle. A $65-per-week legman for Colonel McCormick's newspaper, Lingle never wrote a word—he phoned in his stories to rewrite from the streets. His information was always good because he was on good terms with the cops, politicians and hoodlums who supplied it. Lingle had good connections because while growing up on the West Side, he had the good fortune to become friends with William Russell, who was Big Bill's police commissioner.

Lingle met Capone in 1920, during Thompson's second term in office, while following a story on the murder of James "Big Jim" Colosimo, a gambling boss who was shot to death in his West Side cafe. One of Colosimo's secretaries had said she saw someone running down the street after the shooting—someone who resembled Alphonse Capone.

Lingle let himself be charmed by Capone and never did get to the bottom of the Colosimo killing (in fact, no gangland killing in Chicago—and there have been thousands—has ever been solved by anyone in sixty years). But Lingle did demonstrate what a smart young man could do on a budget of $65 per week. He began to take vacation trips to the gambling spots in Cuba and bought a summer place in Long Beach, Michigan. He also took to wearing a diamond-studded belt buckle given him one day by his friend, Big Al.

He took a suite of rooms in the old Stevens Hotel (now the Conrad Hilton) where he was on a private register. When a house detective was asked about the private register, he became indignant. Mr. Lingle, he said, needed his privacy. From whom? he was asked.

"Why," said the detective, "from policemen calling up to have Jake get them transferred or promoted, or politicians wanting the fix put in for somebody. Jake could do it. He had a lot of power. I've known him for twenty years. He was up there among the big boys and had a lot of responsibilities. A big man like that needs rest."[1]

Lingle once bragged to a fellow reporter, "You know, I fix the price of beer in this town."[2]

As the story goes, Jake got greedy and fell out with his old pals. He gambled heavily at the old Washington Park racetrack on the South Side and routinely dropped a thousand dollars a day on the ponies. He owed a lot of money and it was rumored in the press room that Lingle was using his old pal Chief Russell mercilessly to barter liquor and gambling licenses to Capone's associates.

Sometimes, a man can go too far: On the morning of June 9, 1930, while the rest of the country was settling into Depression, Jake Lingle was heading to the racetrack to drop some cash. He walked east from Wabash Avenue to the Randolph Street underground station of the Illinois Central to catch a train to Washington Park. A cabdriver he knew drove past and shouted, "Play Hy Schneider in the third!"

Jake waved and shouted, "Got him!" and descended the steps to the station just off the Chicago Public Library north entrance.

Two men followed him. One was described later as a blond. Blondie pulled out a .38 and shot Jake in the neck. The world's most expensive newspaper reporter crumpled to the tile floor dead.

Mustering outrage, the *Tribune* offered a $25,000 reward

for the killer of their reporter and ran editorials against the apparent declaration of war upon decent citizens. But when a bevy of out-of-town reporters got on the case the truth about Jake Lingle became more public, and poor old Colonel Robert McCormick had to back down from the pulpit. As usual, the murder was not solved. Crime flourished under Thompson because he worked hand in glove with the criminal element. A year after Thompson took office, the police department was so hopelessly riddled with corruption that the Democratic state's attorney grabbed headlines when he raided City Hall and the mayor's office to find letters to prove the whole department was on the take.

MacLay Hoyne, the prosecutor, was as theatrical as Thompson. A man of great political ambition, he was the only county officeholder to refuse to turn over his patronage to Roger Sullivan's machine system in 1916. Having lost power to Sullivan, he took the coward's way out and became a reformer:

"Newspapers have written that certain Democratic leaders are organizing a local Tammany . . . and that candidates for party nominations in this country will be compelled by a pledge to turn over the power for appointments to some committee," he cried. "I never have, nor will I ever sign such a pledge."[3]

Carried away by his own rhetoric of reform, Hoyne turned his zeal on Thompson, a worthy target. His state's attorney's police presented a splendid spectacle as they swarmed into the connecting offices of the Mayor on the fifth floor at the ornate old Hall and scooped up bundles of papers and files and carted them away.

Thompson bellowed that the raid was "the act of a madman." Hoyne snarled that Thompson was despicable enough to cater to black voters. This "Black Belt politics," he cried, "lets the vicious element in the Second Ward run wild throughout the South Side and other parts of Chicago."[4]

The raid made headlines for weeks, and the charges increased a boiling resentment between the growing Black Belt and the adjacent Irish neighborhoods. The blacks in Chicago were more sophisticated than their rural forebears. Returning Irish vets found black faces in many workplaces that used to be white. Ragtime and jazztime were merging and women of distinction—and color—shopped for the smartest fashions. Blacks were getting heavily involved in real estate for the first time, going into previously white neighborhoods to "bust the blocks," send whites fleeing and property values crashing and then buying up good land at badland prices.

Leadership in Chicago was rarely responsible, unless there was money to be made in it. Men like Hoyne fanned the existing flames of racial hatred, particularly among the Irish. If you could stick Big Bill Thompson with the tar baby of being a nigger lover, you did.

So there was a race riot in 1919. It scarred the soul of the city more deeply than all the scandals that preceded it. The riot began on the South Side when a boy, confined because he was black to the Lake Michigan waters off the beach at 33d Street, swam into the white section of 35th Street. He drowned. It was said he was drowned by white boys who threw rocks at him.

A riot ensued on the magnificent lakefront, in the vast park named for Daniel Burnham. Blacks and whites formed lines in a no-man's-land between the beaches and threw bottles and stones at each other. The riot spread across the South Side and inflamed the parched summer neighborhoods from Bridgeport to South Chicago and the steel mills, to the stinking tenements of Back of the Yards, down through the Black Belt itself.

In the next few bloody days, blacks stormed into white neighborhoods and killed people. They used guns and knives and clubs. Buildings were burned down and women were raped and beaten and left for dead.

Whites stormed into the Black Belt and shot and clubbed men and women to death. Black women were raped and tenements were burned down. It seemed as though the fury would never end.

Reluctantly, Thompson called up the National Guard to put down the riot the police were loath to settle. The Guard came into the tarnished, hateful city and separated the races from their bloodshed. A numbing hatred had possessed the violent people who lived in the violent city and the wound caused the scar that remains today, that cuts through everything in the city's history and politics.

An official commission appointed to look into the causes and preventions of the riot did not face the issue, though it catalogued the facts. In the end, the chief preventive measure agreed upon by the city establishment was never to refer to the riot again. Newspapers, business leaders, community leaders of all races and politicians simply never mentioned what happened in the summer of 1919 until the final, city-shattering black riots in the spring of 1968 forced the memory to be opened.

And Edward Vrdolyak, one of the last lords of the last Machine, would campaign in 1983 and shout angrily, "Don't make any mistake—this is about race!"[5] It was only an election for mayor of a city but he was right: it was about race in 1983 as in 1919. It is impossible to write of racial hatred because it is not the stuff of words, not intellectual, but it is in the bone. It is in the bone still.

THOMPSON WAS AN ABERRATION BUT AN IMPORTANT ONE—HE is the link between the old boodle days of politics and the new day of the impersonal political Machine. He was a Republican but he represented the Democratic link better than any Democrat. Big Bill served three terms between 1915 and 1931 with a four-year vacation in which the "reform" element dithered at the helm.

Chicago entered the roaring twenties at full throttle, scarcely aware of how the city had changed. Chicago had culture and "society" now. The Gold Coast was being established along the North Shore. People were taking their white ties and gowns for an airing in the new Civic Opera house and literature was thriving—no less a savant than Henry Louis Mencken declared Chicago the new literary capital of the United States. *Poetry* magazine was started here and writers like Sherwood Anderson, Ring Lardner, James T. Farrell, Charles MacArthur and Ben Hecht were stirring the wordpot.

The circle of the Loop was broken as tall buildings like the gothic Tribune Tower and the ornate Wrigley Building were erected on Michigan Avenue, north of the river. The river itself—an inconvenient division between the Loop and the wealthy North Side—inspired the building of a series of clever, cantilevered bridges that are among the most beautiful and well-engineered in the world. The south promenade of the river was double-decked and the fruit and vegetable market on South Water Street on the river was moved to the West Side (where it is still called the South Water Market, though there is no water anywhere near it).

Big Bill acquired the nickname of "The Builder" because

he inaugurated the now honored practice of taking credit for every building or project completed for the good of the city. To this day, *no* major building project in Chicago is ever announced by the developer—it is announced by the mayor with a tip of the hat to the developer if he's good. Woe to the developer who jumps the gun—more than one has found himself with a million-dollar plan and no building permit.

Wealth clip-clopped into the city on the hooves of lambs, pigs and cattle. The stink of the stockyards was perfume to the people who lived "back" of the Yards.

The crack streamliners criss-crossing the country had made Chicago the most logical convention center and more political conventions have been held there than in any other city. The city's population was 3.4 million in the thirties and no one knew then that figure would represent its all-time peak. (In 1986 it was just under 3 million and the metropolitan area just under 8 million.)

The Chicago Board of Trade was the biggest exchange outside of New York and there was a magnificent stone building at the foot of LaSalle Street in the financial district of the south Loop to celebrate it. The skyscraper was crowned by a golden statue of Ceres that glittered in the sunlight. The goddess of grain stared across the lights of a still-confident city.

Even the patient city of Chicago had gotten somewhat tired of the clownish Thompson after eight years and, though not directly Thompson's fault, the scar of the riots of 1919 still ached. Thompson must have felt that it might be better not to go for a last hurrah in 1923. He stepped down from the mayoralty.

This action necessitated a few changes in plan and address. For example, Al Capone and his friends moved out of town. Not far out—just across the city limits into Cicero.

With Thompson and his friends out of the way, opportunity was at hand for the Democrats. Roger Sullivan had died in 1920 but not his Machine, which still functioned after a fashion though it had been dangerously damaged. A political machine must control the party by controlling primaries, and that means controlling jobs. Thompson had the lion's share of jobs for eight years. The Irish Machine of Sullivan and Brennan had been weakened by its long fast but, paradoxically, if Sullivan *had* won the mayoralty for the Machine in 1915, it is unlikely it would have survived until the 1980s because the identification with a single ethnic group would have been too close.

To run against Arthur Lender, the Republican candidate, the Sullivan people put up a goo-goo named William Dever, a lawyer with some dangerous reform tendencies but otherwise a decent chap. (Goo-goo is the Chicagoism for the "good government" crowd of reformers.)

Dever was a good enough campaigner to become mayor in 1923 and George Brennan, the schoolteacher from Braidwood with a wooden leg who had fashioned the anonymous machine for Sullivan, became his patronage chief.

As soon as Dever took office, the cracks in the organization showed, in the factionalism, in the rising power of Anton Cermak and the growing numbers of Bohemians who supported him. Though he had been something of a mentor to him, George Brennan feared Cermak.

Cermak had wanted the nomination that Dever got. He had his own clout. He was president of the county board and he had money from the saloonkeepers' association. But Brennan and the Irish didn't think he was right for the job— and they dearly did not want to blow this election.

The arguments against Cermak could be summarized: he was too wet for nominally dry times (which did not make him a hypocrite, at least); he wasn't a Catholic; he wasn't Irish; and some people thought he was a little too close to the dagoes, one of the ethnic slurs used to describe the Capone gang.

Cermak was bitterly disappointed but he stayed a Democrat and he stayed at the door of the Irish Machine office and kept knocking.

Dever, the reformer, was a dud who just didn't have the control. In eight years, Capone and his friends had made deep inroads into the corrupt heart of city government and the police. There was too much money in beer and whiskey and women to let a goo-goo get rid of those things.

An example of Dever's administration is seen in the case of two illegal brewers named Lake and Druggan who were sentenced to a year in jail for being in contempt of a Chicago court. A nominal Republican named Hoffman was sheriff at the time and he saw to it that Lake and Druggan were inconvenienced as little as possible. Their jail quarters were furnished to the nines and they came and went at their pleasure. Hoffman got a thousand dollars a month for bestowing these latchkey privileges, though he was eventually convicted in the matter. (Tony Cermak, fueling more speculation about his ties with Capone, later gave Hoffman a job in the forest preserve district where Hoffman made the same salary for protecting the squirrels.)

Politicians remained friends with the Outfit guys all during the Dever years and after. Some favored pols were even pallbearers at funerals celebrating the sudden demise of this or that gangster. Governor Len Small, a Thompson protégé of the era, gave out so many pardons to Outfit people convicted of this or that trifle that his opponents in the 1924 election made their mocking campaign song "Oh, Pardon Me."

Tony Cermak bided his time for four Dever years, watching George Brennan dispense the patronage, watching the money go to the Irish whom he hated. His time came in 1927 when Big Bill Thompson decided that four years of an ineffectual reformer like Dever would make people sick enough to let him back in.

Cermak decided to get rid of Dever and, in the process, destroy George Brennan and take over the Machine. He secretly gave workers and money to Republican Thompson who, though he was by now a sick man, bloated and blustering, was still the best campaigner the city had ever seen. Both Dever and Brennan knew what was going on but they were fighting for their political lives. The campaign was bloody.

Dever noted Thompson's "America First" campaign theme by saying it was misspelled. What Thompson really stood for, Dever declared, was "Africa First."[6]

The line being drawn in the mud, Thompson crossed it gaily. He brought out the poor old king of England again and beguiled the Irish and Germans another time with his Brit bashing.

The king had muttered something about making an American tour one day and Thompson declared that, as mayor, he would decidedly not welcome the monarch to his city. "If George comes to Chicago," he roared, "I'll crack him in the snoot."

Thompson was now a wet on the Prohibition issue—perceiving more of them in the audience. He swore he was "wetter than the Atlantic Ocean" and that, as mayor, he would "open up ten thousand new places [speakeasies] and take the police away from the task of frisking hip pockets and inspecting refrigerators." Warming up, he pledged that when he was mayor, "No copper will invade your home and fan your mattress for a hip flask."[7]

Thompson created charges and issues out of thin air. In

one of his few acts of reform, Dever had brought William
McAndrew from New York to be superintendent of schools
and clean up the system. McAndrew, from the foreign East
Coast, was the recipient of Chicago hospitality in politics.
Thompson swore that McAndrew was providing tainted history books for Chicago's innocents, "permitting the teaching
of propaganda to the end that the people of the United
States should repudiate the Declaration of Independence and
the doctrines of George Washington."[8]

The most spectacular and bizarre moment in the campaign
came in the primary. Thompson had been abandoned by his
old mentor, Fred Lundin, who supported Dr. John Dill
Robertson in the Republican primary.

Thompson had amiable contempt for old "Dill Pickle"
Robertson, the former health commissioner who now ran the
Municipal Tuberculosis Sanitarium, a patronage job if there
ever was one. But he was savagely angry with Fred Lundin
for opposing him.

Nine days before the primary, he put on a show at the Cort
Theater in the Loop. The theater was owned by U. J. "Sport"
Hermann, an old Thompson pal, and Big Bill was in the
habit of giving rambling talks there on odd subjects at the
noon hour. On this day, signs on the theater announced that
Thompson would present a one act play, "The Rats."

The place was packed.

The curtain opened.

Thompson crossed to stage center with a cage in each hand.
Each cage contained a large, gray rat.

He put the cages on a table and then addressed the rats
before the stunned crowd.

He called the animal to his left "Doc." The other one was
"Fred."

The place exploded into applause.

Thompson waited for the hubbub to die down and then delivered his lines: "Don't hang your head, Fred. That's better now—" Here he prodded the rat with a stick. "Always active. Fred, didn't you send me that cable to Honolulu, and didn't I come back and save you from the penitentiary? Didn't I get the best lawyer in town (Clarence Darrow) to keep you outta jail?

"I knew a year before that you were double-crossing me, but I wanted to live up to the letter of the cowboy code. Don't you think, Fred, in view of all that has happened, that you have earned the name of rat?"

Now he turned to the second rodent.

"Doc, didn't the medical profession and others protest against my plan to appoint you health commissioner? Didn't I stand by you in the face of all opposition, and give you that position? You have circulated the story that I am in bad health and will die soon. Well, Doc, I am not going to die just to please you and Fred."[9]

Thus, Thompson set the tone of the primary and general campaigns. Chicagoans loved it; it was like the bad old days. He won the general election against Dever and the Machine fashioned by Sullivan and Brennan by 83,000 votes. In the process, Thompson destroyed the Dever-Brennan bloc. The beneficiary was Cermak.

Of course, Capone moved back to Chicago, to the Lexington Hotel, and all was as before. The speaks were open as usual and the town was blowsy and voluptuous and everything was in jazztime. The federal government sent a flying wedge of agents to Chicago under the leadership of Eliot Ness to close the city down (his men were called Untouchables because they could not be bribed). They won headlines but nothing changed.

It was as though the city, always raucous but always vital,

had lost its way somewhere around the end of the First World War and was living the life of a tramp. The building boom was dying and would be dead by 1930, not to be revived again until the era of Richard Daley in the late 1950s. No one talked about Chicago becoming First City anymore and the literary lights lit out for New York and Paris. Thompson symbolized a sort of malaise gripping the sick soul. What would come after him? What would change the way things had been for the past fifteen years?

The change was Cermak. The form was the new Machine, the last great Machine in political life in the country.

6
Pushcart

BRAIDWOOD, SIXTY MILES SOUTHWEST OF CHICAGO, IS NOW a half-dead town. It only makes the papers because the electric company is building a giant nuclear power station there. But in the late nineteenth century, it was dirty rich with coal. A company town of mean, unpainted houses, no sidewalks and muddy streets, it was owned, heart and soul and company store, by the Chicago & Wilmington Coal Company. The only people who lived there were those who had to, immigrants who worked for eighty cents a day in the dreary, dangerous, choking coal dust of the mine tunnels.

Out of this black hell came the sturdy, uncouth Anton Cermak. Born in Bohemia, Anton came to Illinois as a child with his parents and many siblings. The Cermak family lived in a frame house two stories high with a coal stove, an oilcloth on the kitchen table and kerosene lamps. There was no living room because every room but the kitchen was a bedroom. The Cermaks worked the mines and kept a cow, pig and a few chickens.

There wasn't much to do in Braidwood but eat, work and drink. Drink was pleasure, the only one. Whiskey Row claimed thirty of Braidwood's ninety saloons, and when he grew up, Tony Cermak was known in every one of them.

The town was divided sharply between Irish and Bohemians with a few Slavs and Germans taking up the rest of the space. The pleasure was as rough as the whiskey. There was pleasure in fighting and Tony fought; pleasure in getting dead drunk and Tony drank; pleasure with girls and Tony took them.

As a teenager, he drove mules in the pits and after hours would relax with his pals in the saloons, one after another. They would buy a pail of beer and pass it around—it was called "shooting the can." The practice numbed the mind until the pain of work was not thought of.

Even in a tough town, Cermak was called Tough Tony. A neighbor remarked that "he was a great lad for joking" but what passed for joking in Braidwood was called violence elsewhere. His jokes ended with him in jail any number of nights. A friend remarked, "When he had a little beer, he couldn't be handled by God, by the boss, by anybody."[1]

"He didn't get along with people," one observer said. "He was always getting into fights. He thought he was a tough guy and could fight. He couldn't leave people alone, and most were scared of him. Girls were very scared. He would always ask to take them home from dances, and they were afraid because he was mean and drunk. He would then lay for the girl and the boy who was walking her home, beat him up, and land in jail. The cop told me he never had to go into a tavern to haul him out. All he had to do was wait by the door, and soon he would be thrown out because he was making trouble."[2]

A restless, brooding man with big eyes in a blank face, thick-bodied and muscular with a tough guy's voice, Cermak was self-reliant because from the earliest age he had done the dirty jobs no one else would do. He asked no quarter and gave none. He was the embodiment of the Machine he would create, the one that would last for half a century.

In 1889, the mule drivers of Cermak's shift in the mine wanted a raise, and Cermak volunteered to take the demands to the bosses. The foreman fired him on the spot. He got another mine job right away but was fired within hours for being "a labor agitator."

If you couldn't work the mines in Braidwood, you had to get out of town. Cermak packed his bag and took the train down to Chicago, where he took a room in his aunt's house in the old Bohemian neighborhood of Pilsen. He got a job working for the streetcar company, driving a horse that helped pull the cars up a steep incline on Blue Island Avenue.

Chicago suited Cermak: he found saloons he liked and was soon back brawling away on Saturday nights, but around 1892 he stopped drifting, bought a horse and started his own business hauling and selling kindling from a wagon. Alluding to this little fact in later years, Big Bill Thompson tagged Cermak "Pushcart Tony."

Nevertheless, by the time the new century dawned, Cermak had six wagons and more than a dozen teamsters working for him. He was married and settled and ran the business out of his own back yard in the heavily Bohemian Lawndale neighborhood. The back yard was his social club as well. His old pals dropped by at all hours for a drink, and when things got a bit rowdy, Tony's mother-in-law would come down the block and break it up. She was tougher than Tough Tony, it seemed.

By now, there were about 200,000 first- and second-generation Bohemians in Chicago. They filled out the area around 26th Street in the old Twelfth Ward south and west of the Loop. The neighborhood was, and is, surrounded by railroad tracks, factories, utility plants and a maze of streets that are made more complex by the intrusion of the Sanitary and Ship Canal. To this day, it is hard to get in and out of the area—and three generations of jurists and lawyers have cursed the name of Anton Cermak who arranged for the criminal courts building and county jail to be built in his neighborhood at 26th and California.

The Bohemians were on the whole a freethinking and intellectually cynical group. Most had little education but, like Cermak, who only went to school for two years, they were smart enough when they had to be.

The Bohemians believed that politics—in Bohemia or Chicago—was really about money. Roger Sullivan could not have put it better than Karel Havlicek, a leader of the nineteenth-century Bohemian freedom movement, who said: "A politician should act very much like a businessman."[3]

The Bohemians were conservative businessmen in Chicago, though their political influence waned in the latter days of the old Machine. In the forties and fifties, most of them migrated out of the city, fleeing the blacks, into Berwyn, a straitlaced suburb west of Cicero and nine miles southwest of the Loop. But when they were concentrated in

Chicago they had power, and the power they had was concentrated finally into the hands of Anton Cermak, the kid from the mines.

THE SUNDAY CLOSING LAW, TO RESPECT THE LORD'S DAY, WAS continuously on the books in Chicago from 1872 until Prohibition—but it was rarely enforced. As we have seen, whenever it was heeded riots developed, uniting Irish, German and Bohemians. The United Societies had been founded in 1906 as a permanent pressure group to fight the Anti-Saloon League and the reform movement. In 1907, Anton Cermak became its permanent executive secretary.

Beer had been brewed in Pilsen since the twelfth century by the Bohemians and so Cermak came by his taste for the stuff naturally. He also had been a driver and errand boy for Fatty Cerveny, agent for Monarch Beer, who in turn worked for the political boss of Lawndale, Adolph J. Sabath. Sabath was a Czech and a Jew and an ally of Carter Harrison, Sr. Cermak worked his way up the political ranks in Sabath's organization as precinct election official, assistant precinct captain and then precinct captain. By 1902, he was chairman of the ward organization.

Cermak was strictly West Side Chicago, which is less prejudiced in its politics than the Irish North and South Sides. He was, therefore, successful in forging alliances between powerful Jewish political interests, including Sabath.

The Chicago Jewish community was in two camps. The older, smaller group of Jews were well established. They lived along the lakefront and identified their interests with German and Protestant reformers.

But the West Side had the larger, later-arriving group of hardworking immigrant Jews from Russia, Poland and other parts of Eastern Europe. They settled around Maxwell Street where it runs into Halsted and worked as peddlers, shop-keepers, haberdashers and tailors. They made a living like everyone else in Chicago—any way they could. In particular, they moved into the costume jewelry trade and worked the midwest by train with their exotic specialties.

"Jewtown," as it was called, was the great open-air market of the city—a vibrant place under the open sky where deals were made by spit and a handshake, where jokes about melt-ing suits were invented and the smells were as good as the babble of sounds.

The Jews of Chicago were politically ambitious and able. The community produced people like Sabath and later Jacob Arvey, who renewed the Machine at a critical juncture after World War II. Jews counted for a lot in the fledgling Dem-ocratic Machine as individuals, but they did not make their political presence felt as a group. Tony Cermak was comfort-able among them and, in fact, became a partner of the wealthy Moe Rosenberg.

Political pundits of a latter day have expressed surprise that a Bohemian like Cermak achieved the ultimate Machine where the Irish had failed, but Tony Cermak's background and inclination gave him advantages. Most ethnic groups did not trust the Irish—and they were right. The Irish were for themselves alone when it came to running politics—at least for a long while—and the Bohemians were less limited in their loyalties. In addition, the Irish would not give a far-thing for a Jew's support; the Bohemians were not so prej-udiced.

Cermak married a Catholic girl, which diluted his unac-ceptable Protestant background, and he raised his kids as Catholics. He had a deep feeling for his family that played well in the neighborhoods.

Cermak worked carefully on his reputation as a trustworthy fellow during the years of his apprenticeship. He joined the clubs and paid the dues. Rivalry with another rising Bohemian leader, Joseph Kostner, was to impel Cermak to throw in with the Sullivan Irish Machine in 1918, but the community in Lawndale always thought well of the tough kid from Braidwood.

Finally, as an outsider in the Irish Machine, Cermak had a certain freedom in choosing his political friends among the Irish power brokers. He did so without incurring the endless hatreds and feuds that often ended the careers of promising young Irish politicos who chose the wrong Irish friends. No one hates a Kerry man as well as a Clare man—but a stranger to Ireland can make friends of them both without being called out on it.

7

Wet Stuff

OVER THE YEARS, ANTON CERMAK HAD LEARNED PATIENCE and how to inspire the trust of others. When Joe Smejkal, a Bohemian wrestler of renown, went up against the Polish Hope, Frank Gotch, in 1912, both fiercely proud ethnic sides agreed upon Cermak as the referee.

In 1902, when he was twenty-nine and already a man of substance, Cermak went to the state legislature from Lawndale. "I was quite nervous when I got there," he said later. "When I took my seat in the House, on my right was a lawyer, and to my left a Harvard man and professor. I was scared to death. In a few days, though, I became less impressed by the others. I believed that I understood people better and had as much common sense."[1]

Cermak outlasted one scandal in the legislature when Republican Senator William Lorimer—called the "blond boss"— was kicked out of Washington on charges that he had bought votes for his election in the legislature (this was before the days of direct Senate election). Cermak was one of the people accused of dealing for Lorimer, and though Tony denied it, the charge kept resurfacing all his life.

Cermak rose steadily in Chicago political circles, becoming secretary of the United Societies in 1907, then Twelfth Ward alderman in 1909, when he took a normally Republican seat. He managed to keep his legislative seat as well, in the great tradition of "double-dipping" in which Illinois pols manage to hold on to two public jobs—and salaries—at the same time.

He was also politically ambidextrous because he was outside the Irish pale in the Democratic ranks: he voted with the Roger Sullivan faction in the state house and with the Carter Harrison faction in the City Council.

On one issue he was consistent: Cermak became the "voice of liquor" in Illinois and wore the banner proudly. He was a dripping wet and used the label to ingratiate himself with the hundreds of ethnic social clubs and their thousands of members who were lubricated to fraternity by the beer they consumed. And he had every politico's dream—a source of income from brewers and distillers that did not have to be accounted for.

Tony also had a manner that appealed to his constituency. "He was very careless (in speech) in those early days," recalled Francis X. Busch, a friend of Cermak's and later the city's corporation counsel. "He appeared tough partially because he wanted to be a contrast to the (upper crust) type of

Dry. He didn't want to seem other than a rough, ordinary guy, speaking for the man on the street. The rougher he was, the more popular he was with his constituency."[2]

Even after he became bailiff of Municipal Court in Chicago—one of many payroller jobs he held—Tough Tony revelled in his association with the underworld class of brewers and distillers.

Cermak, as noted earlier, clashed with Big Bill Thompson over Thompson's 1915 temporary enforcement of the Sunday closing law.

Cermak produced a pledge that Thompson had signed in the past saying he would never enforce the Sunday closing law. The pledge made Thompson the fool—though he was not averse to playing that role. Cermak also bore in on the Thompson nonenforcement of gambling laws—why not stop the card games and policy wheels in the black South Side instead of pouncing on the working fellow's harmless bottle of beer?

On a November Sunday in 1915, Cermak turned out an amazing forty-five thousand people to protest the Sunday ban, and before it was over everyone was having a hell of a good time. The wets marched on Michigan Avenue with signs like "God Put the Sun in Sunday" and "Why Pick on Sunday—the Workingman's Holiday?" Matters were friendly and rowdy—like a typical St. Patrick's Day in Chicago today when the river is dyed green and so is the beer and Polish girls run around in green dresses with buttons that say "Kiss Me, I'm Irish." The silly and happy protest ended up in Streeterville where everyone got drunk because the saloons were always open in this swampy area that was, well into the twentieth century, beyond the official city limits.

Cermak and Thompson were enemies from that day—on

the surface. When it was in Cermak's interest in 1927 to help Thompson beat the Irish Machine, he did so. All alliances in Chicago politics—no matter how sacred—are temporary.

PROHIBITION CAME TO CHICAGO IN THE DRY MONTH OF JULY IN 1919, the same month as the race riot. United Societies and Tony Cermak issued a public statement that they would "fight the old women of both sexes in an effort to retain for the country some semblance of liberty and self-government."[3]

Like many Americans, Cermak was appalled by Prohibition because it offended his sense of reality and seemed to fly in the face of everything known about human nature and economics. He made a prediction: "Chicago may be dry for two months, but not for any longer."[4]

Not even the celebration that doused the saloon lamps the night before the law went into effect could cheer Cermak up. "It was a near beer affair all the way," he said. "When the police begin to act as stool pigeons for the Anti-Saloon League and spend their time in saloons that haven't had any real beer for five days, trying to smell two- and three-quarter percent beer, with the amount of crime that is outside for them to work on, I think it's time to let the people know some things."[5]

Like Daley after him, Cermak was splendidly nonsyntactical but you always knew what he was saying. His message for the voters was the supreme importance of the liquor business to Chicago. He thundered that the city lost a third of its revenue through the dry law. He said the law was an invasion of privacy, an incitement to crime and an insult to the working man.

Cermak had the zeal of a reformer in pursuing every way he could think of to repeal the law—or at least to make a local exception for beer and wine. He got no argument in the thirsty ranks of the City Council. Under his guidance the council opposed expenditure of city funds to enforce the law and once, when an alderman criticized Cermak's wet stand, the other aldermen got up and left the second-floor chamber en masse.

Thompson, in turn, set up his own law enforcement office, paying the Reverend John Henry Williamson ten thousand dollars from his own contingency fund to head the effort. "Let the enforcer take notes," Cermak jeered. "Let him preach against me next Sunday. I'll be there to answer him."[6]

This posturing over a law no one but a few reformers believed in was good politics. Cermak's wet stand earned him plenty of support, and he decided in 1922 to run as the Sullivan-Brennan Machine candidate for president of the Cook County board.

By then, Sullivan had been dead for two years, and it was now Brennan's Machine. Cermak was not particularly a favorite of Brennan's, but they both knew that Prohibition was a national joke (Brennan was the leading wet at the 1920 Democratic National Convention) and Cermak seemed determined enough about running. Brennan was a cut above Cermak in social class, and knew it: by coincidence, Brennan had once been a schoolteacher, though not Cermak's, in Braidwood, while Cermak hadn't made it past third grade. Brennan was urbane, dressed well, went in for witty conversation; Cermak always looked like a roustabout in Sunday clothes even after he started spending some money on suits. Cermak spoke poorly, retaining to the end a habit of pronouncing "hundred" as "hunnert," and some political opponents complained he consumed too much garlic and onions to make intimacy desirable. Brennan's sense of the absurd must have been taxed to its limits at times by this uncouth personage, and he was said to have been the first to take up the matter of reforming Cermak's personal habits.

But clearly Tough Tony had his uses. Brennan let him be slated to run against a true-blue dry named Charles S. Peterson, a goo-goo from the business community whom Cermak called a hypocrite because he didn't want the working man to have his pail of beer though he himself possessed "one of the most thrilling cellars in Chicago."[7]

On their side, the Anti-Saloon League distributed thousands of pledge cards that read: "I realize that if we are to have honest government the people who want it must vote. I also realize that Cermak's wet candidacy makes a special crisis this fall."[8]

The anti-Cermak crowd even got federal help—four days before the election, federal Prohibition agents raided saloons and speaks all over Cermak's home ward. Amazingly, there were open saloons still to be closed, even though the law of the land was now three years old. Cermak railed against the feds and rallied his troops. He beat Peterson, though not by a large margin. With his foot in the door of power, Cermak shoved his whole body through.

The county board had an annoying Republican majority, but a few weeks after the election, one of the Republicans announced that henceforth, he was "with Cermak." It turned out the fellow had a clothing company which suddenly received a rich contract to provide county employees with new uniforms.

Cermak now had money, power and patronage. He was valued for his guts and his attention to detail, and his Irish allies saw ways to make a good thing out of him as president of the county board. But at the same time, they didn't see Tough Tony as a real insider. He wasn't Irish, and that's what counted.

Cermak had his eyes on the mayor's office, and in 1927 he tried to convince Brennan and the other Irish bosses that they ought to back him against Thompson. They turned him down flat and picked Dever instead. Some pols who were there reported that Tony pushed his way out of the room where the slating was held with tears in his eyes. "I'll make those Irish bastards pay for this," he was supposed to have said.[9]

Cermak did not take defeats gracefully. He secretly helped Thompson beat Dever in 1927, and the tactic moved him closer to the source of power in the Machine. With the Irish divided and unable to stand up to Thompson, Cermak was beginning to look like the best thing the Democrats had going for them. His triumph seemed only a matter of time, and Cermak had learned patience along the way. The moment came in 1928.

George Brennan, who had steered the Machine, died suddenly, having made no provisions for a political heir. The now rudderless Irish Machine might have foundered, save for the fact that, miraculously, Brennan had been able to gasp out some instructions to all his Irish colleagues, in attendance at his bedside as he breathed his last. The boys got their story straight and stuck to it. It was the most over-reported deathbed scene since Louis XIV shuffled off the mortal coil, but it ensured that Tony Cermak—despite his broad and growing support among the nonIrish ethnics—had nothing to do with inheriting power.

According to the Irish, Geoge Brennan had gone to meet his Maker bathed in Irish sentiment and, with last gasps, divided power in the party. With a brave smile, Brennan faced eternity and said he wanted that fine Irish lad Michael Igoe to get his post as national committeeman. Mixed with the prayers for the dying, Brennan found breath to say he wanted all the boys to continue supporting Martin J. O'Brien as chairman of the managing committee that handled county patronage.

Who would go against the wishes of the dying boss? Cermak and his supporters. Cermak tested his base of support and thought it was strong—stronger than the story the Irish deathbed attendants were stubbornly sticking to. He had the Jewish leaders with him, including young Jake Arvey and the Rosenberg brothers from the West Side.

The West Siders in Chicago—then and now—are a breed apart from the rest of the city. They are brothers under the skin, despite their ethnic differences. The West Side Irish have more in common with the West Side Italians than with the South Side Irish. They talk the same language and their shared contempt for law is the same. Cermak could count on the West Side, especially because the South Side Irish had overlooked its strength.

Cermak saw that the flaw in the Machine of Sullivan and Brennan was the narrow ethnicity of its base, but he had to wait on Brennan's death before he could move. He had his Irish and Italian support, his Jews and his fellow Bohemians. He had the people who had been left out but he needed the Sullivan-Brennan Irish crowd as well, and he had to find a way to slice into them. Money, as usual, was the answer.

The party was down on its luck and needed cash. One of Cermak's pals was Moe Rosenberg, a West Sider who had become rich after wangling—with Cermak's help—a deal that gave him 90 percent of the utility scrap from Samuel Insull's city-approved power monopoly. Rosenberg now bankrolled Cermak, who distributed the cash to the power brokers of the Irish Machine, believing that greed always overcomes principle.

(After Rosenberg was convicted of tax evasion in 1934, it

came out that he had given some $500,000 to Cermak to bail out the party in the years after Brennan's death. Everyone got a share of the pie but Cermak is said to have held on to $90,000.[10])

The money did induce the Irish to see things Cermak's way about the future of the party. The big break for Cermak came with the defection of Pat Nash from the Irish ranks. Nash was a committeeman and a businessman who believed in the philosophy of making politics pay its own way. A wealthy sewer and construction contractor, he did a lot of business with the state, county and city.

Nash was no Irish sentimentalist. He took a strong liking to the tough Bohemian and admired his skills in attending to the details of running a political organization. Cermak treated politics like business and that appealed to the businessman in Nash. Cermak looked like a good business investment and Pat Nash took a chance with him. As James Denvir, a friend of Brennan's and a true Irishman, said, "Pat Nash delivered the Irish" to Cermak.[11]

For Cermak, the years of waiting were over. A new and shining Machine age was at hand, and he would be the source of power. The incredible had happened—after forty years of largely Irish rule in a squabbling party that never quite succeeded to lasting power, an immigrant from Bohemia whose education had been in the coal mines was now the boss of bosses.

8

Machine

ANTON CERMAK RAN AGAINST BILL THOMPSON FOR MAYOR
in 1931. The country was two years into the Depression
and going deeper. There was a gloom over everything that
couldn't be cured by bathtub gin. Days were as sober as the
lines of the unemployed waiting to get food in a soup kitchen.

In this stark setting, the city of Chicago decided to plan for
another World's Fair, to be held in 1933, to recall the glory
that had come to the city in another time of depression in
1893. This new fair, which did not receive international sanc-
tion, was to be called Century of Progress, and it was to mark
the 100th birthday of the city.

The city was uncomfortable at last with its gangster reputation. There was a restlessness among Chicagoans; they wanted to turn their backs on the past and think of a future that might have hope in it. The fair was a good focus for their hopes.

But what about the mayor of Chicago? How could Chicago look forward while its mayor was nationally known for turning the city over to the Outfit and for presiding over a thoroughly crooked police department while conducting himself like a crude show-off?

The alternative, Tony Cermak, didn't look much better to the town's decent elements. He was an intense Bohemian who had made a career of fronting for the liquor interests. He had the hands of a coal miner and a reputation for drinking and swearing. The city, in search of a World's Fair mayor who would represent all that was good and forward-looking in Chicago, shook its head in confusion.

The Better Government Association stood by Thompson: at least Thompson pretended to be a dry and on the side of law and order. But Cermak had his own reformers. The pioneer settlement house worker Jane Addams, of the West Side's Hull House, announced for him, as did the Hyde Park liberal Charles Merriam and other reformers who were fed up with Thompson. Even ordinary Chicagoans were ready for a change because the mood of the country had changed— the gross venality that was the hallmark of Thompson's style of government could no longer be afforded in an era when men sold apples on street corners.

Thompson made his last hurrah memorable. He reached into a bag of dirty tricks and dubbed Cermak "Pushcart Tony." He made fun of the Irish faction in the Democratic party for letting a Bohemian run their organization, needling the Irish unmercifully. "Something tells me that the Irish are going to tell this Bohunk where to get off," he said.[1]

Cermak came back fighting. He didn't write off any voting bloc in the city as unwinnable. And that included the city's blacks. He went after the black vote with a vigor that was amazing, because the Irish party had never courted the blacks at all, especially since Thompson was so popular in that community.

Blacks made up 7 percent of the city's population now, and they were hurting even more than whites in the Depression. Cermak made it clear, through black spokesmen, that he would provide more jobs and more contracts for blacks while at the same time continuing the old wink and nod to the illegal activities in the Black Belt that existed under Thompson. The policy wheels would grind on; the blind pigs would continue to serve illegal beer; the gambling dens would not be harassed by police.

In one Cermak pamphlet aimed at the black community, a black minister, Reverend Alonzo J. Bowling, put it in more or less plain English: "Abraham Lincoln is not a Candidate in this election.

"The Question, What Has the Democratic Party Done for the Negro, although a stupid one, is a fair one, and is insistently asked. We gladly essay to answer it.

"Most Negroes have always voted the Republican ticket, and are sold to Bill Thompson and the Republican party without an argument . . .

"Do you know that if the Negroes will use their better judgment and divide their votes more largely, the Republicans will give more jobs to hold them and the Democrats to get them?

"The sun of righteous manhood and purity still shines resplendently today as it did in yesteryears. The mayoralty chair of Chicago awaits the step of this child of the common people, now a political, social and economic giant as the

World's Fair Mayor—God has ordained it—the people have decreed it, and this age of Democracy has set its stamp of approval on it. It must be so."[2]

The pamphlet showed again Cermak's attention to detail. He had taken the Machine and he was making it an obedient and powerful force that took nothing for granted and left no vote uncourted, even undergoing an image change for the election in an era before television and public relations. He took to wearing wire-rimmed glasses and put his thick body in dull suits. He called himself "the master executive" in his campaign literature, and when he chided Thompson, he tried to do it with gentleness: "I have no jackasses, no elephants, no rats."

Here was Tony Cermak, the tavern brawler and professional wet, taking as the theme of his campaign "Redeem Chicago." One uplifting bit of literature summarized his life story: "From Illinois Mine Boy to Chief Executive."

Cermak's cause got a last-minute boost when the state's attorney, a week before the election, charged that political payoffs from merchants who wanted to short-weight customers had cost the city fifty-four million dollars.

On Election Day, despite the attention they'd received, the black wards conservatively stayed with the Republicans and Thompson, but they were alone. The white ethnic wards of the city—Irish, Italian, Jewish, Bohemian, Polish and German and all the rest—gave Tony Cermak the seat he had coveted for so long. He won by more than 200,000 votes and Thompson had his first-ever loss.

Tony Cermak was absolutely ruthless as mayor and boss of the now formidable and job-rich Machine. He fine-tuned the political organization every waking moment. The job of Mayor and job of Boss were one.

Cermak honed his image as chief executive. He worked in

his office in the Hall in shirtsleeves with the door open. He took lunch at his desk, usually a sandwich and a glass of milk. He predated Franklin Roosevelt in his skillful use of radio— he had weekly programs he called "intimate chats." The city was charmed by the man and the politicians were dazzled at his skill.

The Depression continued and jobs were hard to come by. Schoolteachers in the public schools were paid in scrip redeemable on the day the system got a fresh infusion of real money. People who had jobs kept working at them even when there was no money to pay them—maybe money would come through some day. The days of jazztime and good times were definitely over, and even patronage jobs were cut back.

Still, every job in the public payroll had its price and it was paid into the coffers of Cermak's Machine. One executive with a civil servant's association described how employees would borrow money from their credit union to buy city jobs. He said a carpenter foremanship went for $750 and it cost $2,000 to buy your way up to be a fire battalion chief.

The official said, "They all hated Cermak's guts. They used to say that 'the bastard is in for what he can get out of it personally.' "[4] Personally or not, the ones who wanted to play had to pay.

Cermak had lost the black vote in the election but he still wanted it. Fifty years later, John "Bunny" East, a Republican committeeman, would recall how Cermak used the cops to get votes: "Cermak was really the father of the ethnic groups being all in one party. I'll tell you how he made the Negroes Democrats: the negroes loved to play whist, they love to gamble a little . . . Cermak put the police department to work. On Friday and Saturday nights, the police stations were crowded with Negroes that had been arrested in gambling raids. And when the aldermen would try to intercede for them, they would be told, 'The minute you people find out there's something besides the Republican party, come back and talk to us.' "[5]

Cermak's genius was in this unceasing push for support, power and votes. He worked for "inclusion" of all groups in one great Machine, smoothing over the ethnic rivalries through the application of the principle that was to guide the party in the decades to come: there's plenty for everybody if we all stick together.

In 1932 the new mayor of Chicago and Lord of the new Machine declared war on crime: "The criminals and hoodlums might as well realize that they must go. The police will put them in jail, or they will put them in the morgue."[6]

Cermak took to going from police station to police station, reporters and photographers in tow, supervising his police, who, he said, were "putting the hoodlums on the run." He picked a troubleshooter from the police ranks, James P. Allman, to be his reform appointment as police superintendent, and the man's Mr. Clean demeanor impressed the City Council. "Gee," one alderman said, "what a man. I offered him a cigar and he looked me over and said, 'I have a cigar,' and reaching into his vest pocket drew forth one."[7]

Cermak had a personal police bodyguard and "special" detail, and its activities were always mysterious. There were rumors in the hall that Cermak feared a hit by the Outfit because it did not want someone so powerful in City Hall. Other rumors said that Cermak worked with Ted Newberry, a North Side gang leader who was supposed to have offered fifteen thousand dollars in 1932 for a hit on Frank (The Enforcer) Nitti. Nitti was Al Capone's cousin and regent of the Outfit, since Capone was in prison by this time on his income tax conviction.

In fact, Nitti *was* ambushed in a hotel room in December

1932, by Richard Lang, a member of Cermak's personal police detail. Nitti did not die. Lang was convicted of assault, and in the course of his testimony he babbled a lot about Cermak. He said Cermak had ordered the hit on Nitti personally and that he was so afraid of the Outfit that he wore a bulletproof vest. It was strange testimony and the trial was bollixed on a technicality. A new trial was ordered for Lang—but it was postponed, and then postponed again. In time, Lang went free.

Was Cermak in sudden war with the Capone gang? He had an abiding connection with the liquor interests, and clearly Prohibition was just about over. When beer was legal again, would its trade be in the hands of the Sicilian mobsters or in hands that were friendlier to Anton Cermak?

The Outfit was pervasive in Chicago politics and Cermak wanted politics in his hands alone. He had bested the Irish, taken over their faltering Machine and made it a great thing. He had a growing national reputation inside the party which saw his technique for binding together ethnic groups as a model for the future. Perhaps Cermak felt he needed to challenge the power of the Outfit in city government, and perhaps he did so in a direct way that the Outfit would understand.

The Lang shooting of Nitti has never been explained to satisfaction. The muddy interpretations that surround it— and Lang's testimony in the trial—are always cited by Chicagoans as a possible explanation for what happened to Cermak just two short years after his rise to become boss of the new Machine.

MATHIAS (PADDY) BAULER, THE RASCALLY ALDERMAN FROM THE North Side Forty-third Ward who figures large in later accounts of the Machine, claimed that it was his idea that

Cermak go to see President-elect Roosevelt in 1933, to try to find money to keep the city running. Cermak had been staying at Paddy's winter home at a time when Roosevelt was on a political trip to Miami.

"Cermak didn't like the son of a bitch, this Roosevelt, and he didn't want to go see the son of a bitch," Paddy recalled. "I says, 'Listen, for Christ's sake, you ain't got money for the Chicago schoolteachers and this Roosevelt is the only one who can get it for you. You better get over there and kiss his ass or whatever you got to do. Only you better get the goddam money for the teachers, or we ain't gonna have a city that's worth runnin'.'

"So he goes over and, Christ Almighty—next thing I hear on the radio is that Cermak's got shot."[8]

Cermak had been in the front seat of the reviewing stand in Bayfront Park in Miami when the President-elect rode by in an open car. Roosevelt waved Cermak to come over and talk to him. They exchanged a few words, and the car was about to pull away when shots rang out. Cermak and four others were hit and Cermak reportedly cried out: "The President! Get him away!" The car shot forward and Cermak fell to the ground.

The newspapers said that Cermak also gasped, "I'm glad it was me instead of him," but the quote rings a bit too perfectly.[9]

Cermak was taken to a hospital, and though the wound was not too bad, it caused an infection at the site of a long-standing colitis condition. Cermak lingered for three weeks in and out of a coma, mumbling about getting money for the schoolteachers. He died in March, just short of two years in power as mayor and boss.

The assassin was Giuseppe Zangara, who was grabbed at the scene. He was a 105-pound, five-foot-five-inch Calabrian immigrant who had been in the United States for nine years. A few days before the attack, he had purchased a .32 caliber pistol for eight dollars. He said he had planned to kill outgoing President Hoover, but when he read Roosevelt would be in Miami, he changed his plans.

Zangara babbled during his trial about his hatred of officials and especially Presidents. He was given a speedy execution and that was the end of it—save that to this day, some Chicagoans believe that the wild Italian had really been commissioned to assassinate Cermak to avenge the shooting of Nitti.

Cermak's body was returned to Chicago where it lay in state inside City Hall. Chicagoans filed past and stared at the mortal remains of Tough Tony. A certain sobriety fell over the city—Cermak surely had been someone special.

But not everyone was reverent about his passing. As one of the police guards at the casket recalled, a city employee came up and stared at Tony's closed eyes for a long time. Why was he staring? asked the cop.

"I wanna make sure the bastard is really dead."[10]

9

The Cash Machine

THE DEATH OF CERMAK CONFIRMED THE STRENGTH OF THE new Machine. The coalition he had put together did not fall apart without him. The boys forged on, the Machine was still in business.

Pat Nash, chief among Cermak's lieutenants, moved quickly to reassure the Irish as well as the Bohemians and Jews that the pies would be cut the same way they had been under Tony's leadership. Nash was seventy years old and very rich. He had been running patronage for Cermak as head of the county board and he did not want the job of mayor as well. John Clark, a bright young alderman from the West Side, *did* want it, but because he was perceived as too smart and too ambitious, he was not trusted by the other Irish.

Nash needed a front man as mayor, someone not too greedy, not heavily involved in the infighting and who would leave patronage control and other important matters to Pat. While he was at it, Nash also figured to find someone who could speak English better than Cermak, someone with a little polish to him.

He found Edward J. Kelly, then chief engineer of the Metropolitan Sanitary District, whom he brought in as the "sanitary candidate." Governor Henry Horner, a Machine ally, quickly signed some legislation that allowed the City Council to pick a successor to fill out Cermak's term without an election. Kelly became mayor without a vote being cast and the Machine was running smoothly again. (Kelly should have been grateful to Horner but he was not. They had a falling out years later when Horner vetoed a favorite Kelly bill to legalize handbooks and the neighborhood bookie. Kelly opined then that Horner "as a governor would make a good hod carrier."[1])

Kelly was an odd choice for Nash to make. He had been in the corrupt Sanitary District for years, and a series of scandals in the 1920s had splashed mud on the sanitary engineer. He was even under indictment for a time for involvement in selling of dredging and hauling contracts, but though the state's attorney was then a Republican, Kelly escaped major harm by showing that he was nowhere as guilty of taking money out of the district as others were. The prosecutors left him alone, and the indictment was quashed before trial. This ability to fall into excrement and come out with the odor of a rose was to stand Kelly in good stead in his new job.

Kelly did have one bonus he brought to his job—and to the Machine he served. He was a longtime pal of Robert

Rutherford McCormick, the original and eccentric owner of the *Chicago Tribune*. When McCormick was twenty-five, he had served as president of the Sanitary District board and brought to the job the kind of reforming zeal that later would see him trying to steer the English-speaking world into phonetic spelling. His reforming bent for language lasted longer than his stint as a Sanitary District reformer—the *Tribune* was still spelling words like tho and thru and frate in the 1960s.

The story of the friendship between the garrulous Kelly and the oddly shy McCormick explains the immunity Kelly had from attacks by the *Tribune* in the decade that followed. Pat Nash would be chopped up in *Tribune* editorials and *Tribune* cartoonists would lash everyone in the Machine— except Kelly.

It seemed that when McCormick went to work at the Sanitary District as an elected official, he decreed that merit selection would prevail in jobs and not political clout. It was an odd thing to decree, but no one expected such a ruling to last long or even to be observed.

McCormick one day spotted a young foreman in the district tell a slacker to get busy. The man, doubtless with connections, told the foreman to get lost. The foreman knocked him down. McCormick was delighted—he favored the direct approach himself in employee relations. He marked down the foreman's name as someone worthy of promotion: Edward J. Kelly.

A few days later, however, Kelly submitted his resignation to McCormick.

"What's this for?" asked the Colonel.

"I'm a Democrat, you're a Republican," Kelly said. "I'm quitting before you fire me."

"Go back to work," McCormick said.[2] And that was that. They became good friends on the job and off. Ralph

Berkowitz, a longtime Chicago Republican, said that the two of them spent their evenings together and Kelly took a lead in introducing McCormick to young ladies he knew. The deeply reserved McCormick needed all the social help he could get. He was grateful and—as others testified—he was a good friend and a lasting one. Years later, when Kelly was being investigated for tax evasion, McCormick made it a point to invite Kelly to lunch with him at the prestigious Chicago Club, demonstrating his friendship before the assembled business leaders dining in the great hall.

Kelly was to the city payroll born. His father had been a fireman and, in keeping with tradition, ran a saloon on the side. Kelly himself had been an undertaker's assistant for a time, before going "on the district" as the boys put it.

The Sanitary District's official function is to flush away Chicago's sewage. Since 1900, when Chicagoans dredged out the Chicago River to reverse its flow and turn it into a sewer to carry waste *away* from Lake Michigan, Chicago's sanitary planners have always thought big. There have always been big construction contracts, hauling deals and bonding opportunities available at the District; it works on the dull, invisible underside of city political life, and hence has always been a favorite spot for Machine politicians with a taste for graft. The district also offers a wide range of just those kinds of low-level jobs that are most valuable to the Machine.

The practice of handing out District sinecures to people who have made themselves politically useful is so well understood that it is rarely necessary even to lie about the practice. A Brennan protégée, Elizabeth Conkey, who headed Machine women's groups for years, once explained at a hearing into District corruption that of course she had never actually done much work for the District, which paid her three hundred dollars a month as an investigator. "I told

Mr. Brennan that my husband couldn't afford to pay my expenses of going to the Houston (Democratic national) convention and of travelling around the state in the interests of the party. I told him I wanted a job so I could earn my political expenditures." It had been understood, she explained, that of course she was not going to be spending much time at the District.[3]

In the "whoopee era" scandals that rocked the District, it was said that the District had paid out some seventy-two thousand dollars in one year for young ladies to accompany executives on rides about the city. The ladies' services were arranged by a woman who was on the District payroll. The mud from all of this spread throughout the Machine, but Kelly seems to have escaped the worst of it. Others went to prison. Kelly seems merely to have gained an education.

Kelly knew how the Machine was supposed to be working even before he became mayor, and it ran as smoothly under his guidance as under Nash. In fact, it ran better. Under Kelly, the take from Machine workers was systematized. The kickbacks became subtle—an employee was supposed to buy so many tickets to a fundraiser for his boss or contribute so much to a campaign fund or maybe a Christmas fund. Years later, disgruntled employees in the Jane Byrne administration were to charge that anyone making over twenty thousand dollars a year was expected to kick back one thousand dollars to the reelection fund of the boss.[4] The Machine did business with outsiders and with itself.

A ward committeeman told a University of Chicago graduate student in 1952 the facts of Machine politics: "What I look for in a prospective precinct captain is a young person—man or woman—who is interested in getting some material return out of his political activity. I much prefer this type to the type that is enthused about the 'party cause' or all 'hot' on a particular issue. Enthusiasm for causes is shortlived, but the necessity of making a living is permanent."[5]

And it was never the high-paying, clean office jobs that yielded the most. People who can qualify for that kind of job probably do not need the Machine enough to provide it the kind of loyalty it requires. Alderman Edward Vrdolyak was to remark in the 1970s that his most valuable precinct captains were low-paid sanitation workers. That is why Chicago kept four-man garbage trucks into the 1980s. The work of the Machine is hard, and it is not pleasant, and not everyone wants to do it; that is why it has paid off so handsomely for those who do.

During the Kelly years such devices as the annual ward party ad book, through which local businesses were solicited for funds, and the officeholder's annual "golf day" were brought to perfection. Such occasions provided an opportunity for the loyal workers of the Machine to drink a lot of beer, play eighteen holes of golf—and leave a surplus for their "chinaman's" campaign fund.

It was job procurement, however, that was the steady source of income, as well as of precinct workers for the elections. Getting a job was no guarantee you would keep it if you didn't get out the vote in your precinct. For example, William J. Connors, committeeman of the North Side's Forty-second Ward, estimated that his ward maintained 350 to 500 public jobs in the early 1950s. The public payroll of his Democratic workers in the ward totaled about $1.32 million per year.[6]

There were fifty wards in the city then as now in addition to thirty township committeemen controlling jobs in the rest of Cook County, in the suburban areas old Chicago pols still call "the country towns." By the end of the Daley years, there were at least thirty thousand patronage jobs controlled by the city Machine, not counting the "civil service" jobs that could still be influenced in the police department and fire department and in other quasi-civil service agencies.

The Machine worked itself quickly into the fabric of Chicago life in the 1930s because it could provide the jobs no one else could. These were desperate years when people doubled and tripled up in apartments and dodged the landlord while looking hopelessly for work. Welfare was an invention of the future. Government relief was direct—mostly food—and was for today alone. The struggle to survive made people appreciate the favors of the Machine, which were delivered by the precinct worker, the lowliest and most important cog in the Machine. There were three thousand precincts in Chicago, mini-neighborhoods inside neighborhoods, and they were all manned by loyal Machine hands who, in addition to recommending people for jobs, brought food, relief and friendship up the back stairs of the tenements. They gave valuable favors and expected votes in return. Issues? Reforms? The Machine took care of people in a way that the private agencies could not and that the government still resisted. The Machine never had much of an ideology. It was the public version of the private corporation.

The Machine helped to lift Chicago out of the mud of Depression. In so doing, it developed a lifelong alliance with the Chicago business community that would set it apart from other Machines in the country and would account, in great part, for its longevity.

Not only those businesses with a need for city contracts were loyal to the Machine. The corporations in Chicago had need of their precinct captains as well.

Reminiscing about the Kelly years, Ralph Berkowitz explained it this way: "There's such a thing as a permit, parking privileges, zoning—all sorts of things a mayor can do for you.

"If the State Street merchants want an especially heavy

police patrol up and down the street, or if they want a subway tunnel that leads from the El into Marshall Field's store, those are things that you can get from your mayor and he's your guy.

"You don't borrow trouble. I only know of one business that paid one hundred percent personal property tax in Chicago in the old days and that was Sears Roebuck under Julius Rosenwald. He wouldn't go along. He paid. That was the only outfit. The rest of them didn't pay. There are so many advantages. Tax breaks. There's a million things the mayor can do for you."[7]

Even if you liked to pay taxes, there were plenty of other things the Machine could do for you. Sears was glad to get federal Model Cities money in the 1960s to preserve its West Side headquarters from an encroaching black slum; the Machine worked that out with the feds. In Chicago good politics is good government is good business.

THE PARTNERSHIP BETWEEN POLITICAL MACHINE AND BUSINESS community worked in subtle ways as well. Patronage did not have to stop with government jobs. There were jobs in businesses that owed a favor to this or that Lord of the Machine. Obtaining a job in the private sector for a political friend didn't involve coercion—it was probably not even illegal.

An old-time Chicago resident described how it worked: "In 1938, when I graduated from Crane Technical High School, I applied for a job with Sears, Roebuck Company's mail order house, whose headquarters was located in the Twenty-fourth Ward. . . . The employment office refused to give me an application. My precinct captain then secured a letter from Alderman Jacob M. Arvey of the Twenty-fourth Ward, in which I lived. Upon presentation of the alderman's letter, the Sears employment office promptly produced a job application for me."[8]

Contracts were the main source of Machine wealth. Working on the scale model provided by Roger Sullivan and George Brennan and perfected by Anton Cermak, the Machine did business with itself. If you were a Machine regular, you might have an insurance company on the side that handled city insurance. If you were a Machine power, you had a construction firm or a law firm that did city business.

John J. Touhy, county commissioner in 1949, was also a partner in an insurance business with Alderman Harry Sain. He explained: "We handle a lot of business, no question about it. I assume it's just good business in the ward to carry insurance with us."[9]

Chicago gradually became an airtight and cozy little corporation in the three decades between 1931 and 1961. There were insiders and there were outsiders and the faces never changed. Alderman Harry Sain passed on, and his kid, Ken Sain, became Daley's vice mayor—a ceremonial post that led to consulting contracts. Everybody knew everybody else and everybody helped everybody else out.

Certain companies, then and now, did business with the city all the time, winning the same construction contracts year after year, the same plumbing contracts, the same heating contracts, the same school supply contracts.

Want sealed bids? You got them: during the years when Edward J. Kelly was chief engineer at the Sanitary District, the Underground Construction Company used to get a lot of district business. There was a bridge to be built at Crawford (now Pulaski) Avenue and the company made a bid. All the bids were sealed. The company bid $343,315 for the job. A rival contractor submitted a bid of $266,275. By law, the district had to take the lower bid.

But when the sealed envelopes were opened, the Underground Construction Company was found to be low bidder at $264,950. The award might have gone unremarked except that an independent auditor, examining the records a few months later, looked into the envelopes and found two pieces of paper in the Underground envelope—one with the higher figure, one with the lower.

(Underground got the job despite the fraud. Later, when it couldn't do the job for the low bid, it asked for cost overruns—and got them.)

It may not be unrelated that Kelly himself, in his years at the district, had an annual salary of $15,115, though he reported an average income of $72,436 per year.

The all-knowing and all-seeing Machine ran the city like a vast corporation. It was more than the sum of its parts or the popularity of whoever happened to be its head. The money was rolling in despite the Depression. Every public good was turned to private profit; every necessity of making a city work made someone rich.

The system was fine-tuned in the years of the Kelly-Nash rule of the Machine (critics called it the Nelly Cash machine). The thirties and the forties were rich years and the relative economic weakness of the city only increased by comparison the Machine's strength.

In 1950, Paddy Bauler was the boss of the Forty-third Ward and owner of a saloon called the DeLuxe Gardens. He sat still for an interview with *New Yorker* writer A. J. Liebling, who later incorporated the chat into a series of unflattering stories about Chicago that were collected in a book called *The Second City*.

Bauler told Liebling the facts of Machine life. In his ward, he said, he had 40,000 votes. Those votes were the responsibility of his seventy-six precinct captains. Each captain had a public payroll job with the city, county or state.

"We have some very nice jobs to give out, from $270 to $350 a month," he said. "And all the fellow has to do is keep track of the votes in his precinct and get out the Democratic vote when it counts. The way he does that is by knowing everybody in his precinct and being nice to them. Everybody needs a favor sometimes, but some people are too dumb to ask for it.

"So I say to my captains, 'If you notice a hole in the sidewalk in front of the fellow's house, call on him a week before the election and ask him if he would like it fixed. It could never do any harm to find out.' When you got a good precinct captain, you got a jewel."[10]

REFORMERS SEEMED CONTEMPTUOUS OF THIS GRITTY PERSONAL approach to government (which is why reformers did so badly in Chicago), but it had been practiced even in nineteenth-century Chicago. A reformer of the time, observing the work of a Democratic precinct captain he called "Farmer Jones," said Jones had a lot of potential Italian voters in his precinct but did not know the language. So he found a bright eight-year-old girl, daughter of a ward resident, who did speak Italian. He made friends with her, bought her candy and toys and ingratiated himself with her family. When Election Day rolled around, he got her parents' permission to use her as a translator. Led by the little girl, he went around to his Italian constituents and had her explain that he was a man willing to do favors for them—even bribe them—in exchange for their votes.

The reformer was horrified by the vote buying but admiring of the zeal of the precinct worker: "Which of all the churches, I wondered, would take so much trouble for so long a time merely in order to get hold of a little Italian girl to work into their organization this rough, unassimilated hunk of Italianism which 'Farmer Jones' had got hold of in order to strengthen the Democratic Party?"[11]

As Dunne's Mr. Dooley noted, "A reformer tries to get into office on a flying machine. He succeeds now and then, but the odds are a hundred to one on the lad that tunnels through."[12]

The Machine expanded greatly in the fifteen years that Nash and Kelly ran it, and it ran with sophistication. There were big deals made with big businessmen—but the simple origins of the Machine's strength were not forgotten. Every job on the public payroll was owned by a man who was beholden—not just to a sponsor or "chinaman"—to the whole organization that created the job. And the way to show your gratitude was to get out the right vote every Election Day.

The Machine had outgrown its ethnic base and it had taken a non-Irish ethnic—Tony Cermak—to expand its appeal. Now, in these critical years of growth, it would finally complete the linkup Cermak had envisioned with the growing black community. A generation after the 1919 race riot, the black city remained separate, but, as we shall see, it was also incorporated into the Machine.

10
The Other Big Bill

THE BLACK BELT WAS A NARROW NEIGHBORHOOD THAT
gradually filled out the Second Ward on Chicago's near
South Side. From this ward came Big Bill Thompson and his
friend George Harding, two white men with close ties to the
black community. Though the ward had been 27 percent
black as early as 1910, the community still struggled for its
own representation in the City Council.

In 1914, George Harding retired as senior alderman in the
ward and Oscar DePriest, a black ex-county commissioner,
stepped into the race for the office. After he won and became
the first black alderman in the city, he became a hero who

was surrounded by admiring throngs whenever he strolled down the main thoroughfares of the Second Ward.

DePriest was a hustler and a Thompson stalwart, and it paid off. His housepainting business prospered, and he also made money buying buildings cheap on the edge of the Black Belt and moving black tenants into them. Over the next few decades DePriest's "busting-the-blocks" technique was to become a major source of revenue for people with the right government connections. The beauty of it was that it perpetuated itself: each new busted block created a new fringe area of panicky whites, and whole neighborhoods could be turned over in a matter of months.

DePriest ran into trouble when, in 1917, he was indicted by MacLay Hoyne, the Democratic state's attorney, for helping gambling houses, gamblers and whorehouses.

At his trial, DePriest admitted taking money from the black gambling boss Teenan Jones to keep the cops away from his elite "black and tan" resort on South State Street. He also admitted getting police detectives demoted "to harness" through his City Hall connections when they threatened his gambling friends and pimps. Despite these admissions on the stand, a jury—doubtless stunned by his honesty—returned a verdict of "not guilty." (DePriest was a political pioneer despite—or because of—his questionable associates. He was to be the first black on the Cook County board—picked by the mini-Machine of Bill Lorimer; the first in the City Council; and, in 1926, the first black congressman in the U.S. House of Representatives, all from a power base in the old Second Ward of Chicago.)

DePriest's successor as alderman was Louis B. Anderson, another supporter of Bill Thompson and Fred Lundin. He was returned to the Council eight times, and he was an effective representative—as the Municipal Voters' League pointed out, "In his mellifluous way, he is quite as bad an alderman as was his predecessor, DePriest. . . . He is known as a friend of gamblers and divekeepers. . . ."[1]

As their white counterparts had done in the days before the Machine, black politicians went after power and money in a hit-or-miss fashion. DePriest, Anderson and others had no real system for ensuring their retention in the political positions that offered them such personal profit. They owed their careers to the concentration of black votes in the Second Ward and mutually profitable relationships with white politicians. A system to keep them in power was to be devised by William Dawson, the man who helped lead the black people of Chicago not only to the Democratic side but right into the heart of power of the Machine.

A poor Georgia boy, Dawson came up to Chicago and hustled for a living in the Second Ward. Though he was a Republican, he admired DePriest, but he also saw a need for more sophistication in politics. One of his first principles was not to challenge white authority—as DePriest loudly did— but to work with it to control black neighborhoods. This attitude made him a trusted adviser on black affairs in white councils and helps explain the immense power he was allowed to accumulate as the black community in Chicago grew. As part of his political apprenticeship, Dawson served two terms as alderman from the by now all-black Second Ward from 1933 to 1939.

The country was seven years into the era of Franklin D. Roosevelt, and the Democrats were still patching together the ethnic and racial coalition that would keep them in power for decades. A true racial coalition did not yet exist in the party in Chicago. Dawson and many other black leaders were

Republican, as was the ward organization. Republicans were still riding on the legacy of Abraham Lincoln, even in the Black Belt of Chicago.

By the late 1930s Edward Kelly decided that the immense black vote had to be harnessed if the Machine was to keep growing and solidifying its hold on the city, county and state. The problem was how to bring the blacks into the fold without alienating ethnic whites who despised them.

A "race man" like Oscar DePriest—who strutted his blackness and defied white authorities—could not effect the reluctant marriage, but Kelly liked what he saw in the careful, quiet politician named Dawson.

Dawson lost a power struggle in 1939 and with it his job as Republican Second Ward alderman. Kelly approached him sometime around 1940 or 1941 and asked him to change parties, become a Democrat and become the boss of the Second Ward as committeeman. Dawson saw his chance, and he took it. He became the boss of Bronzeville, as Chicago's black areas were called then, and in 1942 was elected congressman from the Second Ward, the job that had once belonged to DePriest.

Boss Dawson served in Congress until his death in 1970 and was simply the most powerful black political boss in the country in his time.

Like Nash, Kelly and Cermak, Dawson believed in organization and had an unending respect for the calculations that add up to power. He built his organization up block by block over the years. Though he talked a great deal about his people—black people—and their needs and ideals, his first question of anyone who walked into his ward office was a practical one: how many votes can you deliver?

He was a pragmatist who believed that politics was about money. As a result, he could speak the same language to blacks and to his white comrades in the Machine. Once he was challenged by some black leaders from the ward who accused him of being an Uncle Tom because he did not speak out about bad housing and poor city services in black areas. Dawson listened to the reformers for a time in his office and then said:

"Mr. Leader, how many precincts do you control?"

The leader of the reform group assembled appeared confused.

Dawson sneered. "You haven't got anything but a loud speech and a lot of threats. Go out and get yourself an organization with a lot of people. Then come back to see me, and we can work out something. Meanwhile, get out of my office. You're wasting my time."[2]

The Dawson Machine inside the larger Machine was formidable. Dawson was a powerful speaker but he saved his rhetoric for the pros—his best speeches came at closed-door meetings with his precinct captains or before the Democratic central committee. "I feel a speech comin' on," he would cry like a Baptist preacher calling the faithful, and his speeches would be litanies of rhythmic poetry, praising not the Lord but the Machine. In closing his ward meetings, he would stare down at his faithful precinct workers and intone: "Walk together, children, and don't get weary."

Civil rights was never on his local agenda. He dismissed the rhetoric of the 1960s with rhetoric of his own: "You want oratory, don't you? Well, let me tell you something. The world is full of orators, but it isn't full of organizers. In this Second Ward, we've got organizers. I don't need to make speeches to get out the vote."[3]

Dawson's precinct captains reaped all the rewards of their hard work, for his ability to obtain patronage jobs from the Machine was legendary. In 1946, when Dawson won in an off-year election that was otherwise a Republican sweep, a reporter asked Dawson why he won. The Congressman seemed amused. "Just put in your little story that Bill Dawson's machine rolled again," he said.[4]

Dawson had the worst absenteeism rate of any Illinois Congressman but explained that he had to spend a lot of time in Chicago to "take care of my people." His example in missing roll calls in Congress would be followed later by one of his disciples, August (Gus) Savage, a Second Ward congressman who achieved the absolutely worst absentee record of all 435 congressmen.

How did Dawson take care of his people? The evidence is clear: by getting jobs for them. Dawson controlled thousands of jobs in national government and in Chicago and Cook County. He had a particular reputation for being able to get jobs and promotions in the Post Office.

Dawson was as cynical as any of the other Machine lords— he was the spiritual brother of Roger Sullivan and George Brennan and Anton Cermak. He made no attempt to conceal his financial relationship with the illegal policy wheels that operated openly in the ward. As one prominent black leader explained this policy-politics connection: "Now, if I were to run for a political office, I would have to raise campaign expenses. If I went to every professional man in the town, I would not be able to raise two hundred dollars. But if I went to the vice lords and policy kings, I would get two or three thousand from a couple of them."

Known as numbers in other cities, the game apparently was called policy in Chicago because the numbers runners were like the insurance policy men who came around each week to collect a dime on burial policies. During the Kelly years, there were about twenty-five policy wheels in Chicago's black wards. They were protected by Dawson, who said that if money was going to be made out of the black community, then black people ought to make it.

Each player would give the policy writer a set of numbers along with a bet. A nickel bet on the right combination might make you a five-dollar winner.

The drawing was always held in a public place and was sort of a free show for the neighborhood. Usually seventy-eight numbers were put into a "wheel" or barrel and twenty-four numbers were chosen by lot. The numbers were posted in two columns of twelve numbers each, and if a player's slip contained three numbers that appeared in one column, he won one hundred times the amount of his bet.

The odds of winning were small, estimated in the 1930s by University of Chicago professor Harold N. Gosnell at 1 in 174. But in a hard life the game was something to dream on. Indeed, to this day, there are various "dream books" sold in black neighborhoods all over the country in which dreams are translated into numbers that can be played in that day's lottery. (The illegal policy wheels have been largely supplanted by the legal and wildly successful state lottery. When the lottery bill was in the Illinois house, one of Dawson's protégés—Representative Harold Washington—argued that policy wheel operators should be hired to run the lottery because they had the necessary "expertise." His argument was turned down.)

Black life in the urban ghetto was stark and depressing. Jobs were few, and even middle-class blacks in Chicago can remember times when a job as a policy writer stood between a family and starvation.

Many blacks lacked either education or an understanding of the impersonality of city life. Even if you lost, policy offered solace and connection to powerless people who needed to believe in luck and magic.

"Not bad, for twenty cents a day to always have something on your mind," one black told Gosnell in the bleak thirties.[6]

Around the policy wheel there flourished an enchanted world given over to the interpretation of dreams and feelings. A black businessman recalled: "An attempt to capitalize on bad dreams created a dream book industry that is still not well known outside the black community. There were more than twenty dream books. . . . The most popular during the twenties and thirties were *The Three Witches, The Gypsy Witch, The Japanese Fate, Aunt Della's,* and *Aunt Sally's.* These books were best sellers whose popularity was exceeded only by the Bible in the black community.

"Dream books translated the meaning of a dream into policy numbers, which were usually a combination of three numbers. For example, a dream of Death Row translated into 9–9–29, and the name Henry translated into 27–32–33."[7]

Because the sums bet on the policy wheel were so small, there were a great number of "writers" who scattered through the neighborhoods to collect wagers. A successful wheel usually employed about three hundred writers, so that during the Kelly-Nash years an estimated six thousand people were making daily canvasses for prospects throughout the South Side black neighborhoods.[8]

It was a ready-made organization, and Bill Dawson learned a lot from it. Just as the policy kings built their fortunes nickel by nickel among people without money, Dawson built his political organization vote by vote among people without power. Neither project was easy, but both were enormously successful, so successful that John and Robert Kennedy, planning a run at the presidency during the late 1950s, came to talk to Dawson's lieutenants. Their notes on the Dawson technique for building support appeared in a Kennedy campaign manual that went out to workers all over the country.

As Edison Love, a Dawson captain recalled: "They were two excited young men. They spent nearly an entire morning picking our brains, jotting down every word we said about how to organize."[9]

Cermak had recognized early on that policy and politics were married in black wards. He started chipping away at Republican strength in black wards as early as 1932—though someone like Dawson would not be "converted" until Ed Kelly went after him on the eve of the Second World War.

Cermak's approach was brutal. He said that the "decent people in the Negro community" were asking him to wipe out the policy wheels because, in the Depression, "colored people are near starvation and these thieves under the pretense of operating games are taking their nickels and dimes."[10]

The message was loud and clear to the policy wheel kings, particularly the famous Jones brothers—Eddie, George and McKissick who owned homes in Mexico City and Paris. They were Thompson allies but they understood where their new allegiance lay. They shifted gears and got out the vote in 1933 for a Democratic candidate for alderman. The policy games were left alone.

Dawson's organization was full of bright and ambitious men, including the Olympic runner Ralph Metcalfe who had had a starring role with Jesse Owens in the 1936 Games in Berlin. Metcalfe was to succeed Dawson after his death. He was a loyal Machine player until the civil rights pressure generated by people like Martin Luther King, Jr., reached Chicago and grew too great for him to ignore. He then switched to the ranks of the reformers and declared himself free of Machine control. But the Dawson Machine had been built up piece by piece, and it would not be quickly dismantled when one individual had a change of heart.

Another bright young man in Dawson's organization was Harold Washington, later to become mayor of the city. Washington was one of a new generation of blacks who had served in the Second World War, felt the sting of prejudice outside their communities and returned to Chicago determined to play a bigger role in the life of the city. Washington's father had been a precinct captain in the old Third Ward organization of Mike Sneed, a black leader whose organization was absorbed into the Dawson steamroller. Like other talented black men of his generation in Chicago, Washington enrolled in Roosevelt University and got his education from an institution founded with money gained from outspoken liberals and reformers like Marshall Field III. But once he had gotten that education, the only place for Washington to exercise it was inside the Dawson machine.

Dawson constructed a truly pragmatic kind of black politics which contrasted sharply with the personality or issue-based politics practiced in other parts of the country. But Dawson had his emulators. Chicago was developing the wealthiest and most diverse black society in the country in the Dawson years— the census claims that the black middle class of Chicago today is the largest in the nation, and four of the top twenty-five black corporations in the country are headquartered there.

Dawson brought blacks into the Machine by adapting its strategies and techniques to the needs of his own community. The black community gained jobs and business, just as any other group inside the Machine did. The deal was, until very recently, mutually satisfactory. Given the climate of the city, blacks were grateful for the benefits they did receive and believed they could not do much better under another kind of political leader. And the growing black population pulled the right levers on Election Day, delivering a crucial and rock-solid margin that kept the Machine in power.

11

Second City

THE CITY NEVER ACHIEVED WHAT IT THOUGHT IT WOULD when the new century turned. During the years when the Machine formed itself, grew and wove itself into the fabric of society, the city stagnated. Between 1930 and 1955, the Loop declined and the skyline remained unchanged. The Machine grew—but it remained as it was formed, a hard-bitten and cynical institution built on jobs and favors and taking its percentage of whatever action was going on. It operated on the fixed idea of the breadline and the poverty of the streets. It did not develop breadth until it was too late.

Chicago faced reality in the 1930s. It was not going to be the greatest city in the country. The tremendous growth was over. The city was as big as it was going to get—though it would keep expanding as a metropolitan area by adding suburbs all around itself.

The "gee whiz" attitude of the 1920s was turning into a sour "What the hell" by the 1940s. Contrast the attitude of the *Chicago Tribune* of the 1920s when it proclaimed itself daily as "The World's Greatest Newspaper." At regular intervals, the paper ran a "program for Chicago" on its editorial page and the first goal of the program was to "Make Chicago the First City of the World."

In A. J. Liebling's 1952 articles for *The New Yorker,* he wrote: "The hopes for all-around pre-eminence, to come as an automatic bonus for being biggest, have faded. . . . Still, the habit of purely quantitative thinking persists. The city consequently has the personality of a man brought up in the expectation of a legacy who has learned in middle age that it will never be his."[1]

It was not only Chicago that failed to live up to its early promise. The entire country had changed since the Depression and World War II. The automobile was now within reach of most people and as a result the suburbs flourished. As the whites left the cities, the nonwhite urban population grew. More important, the economy improved. The Machines were built on the ideas of jobs and graft, but in an economy with almost full employment and an educated, upwardly mobile population, it was hard to maintain voter loyalty. A precinct captain could offer few favors to a man who had a job, a car, an education and his own home. The quality of people attracted to the often gritty life of the political machine declined.

Why did the Machine in Chicago last so long then? First, there was the iron rule of Boss Bill Dawson in the black community. Dawson got a grip on the tens of thousands of blacks from the rural South who flooded the city after the war, and he made them his own. The new wave came with little eagerness to take on the challenges of their urban lives. They came looking for jobs. There were jobs, but not enough, and so the welfare system was born: Both jobs and welfare flowed through Dawson. Dawson's success and the wards delivered by the traditional underworld elements of the West Side formed a core of eleven solid wards that made the Machine unbeatable.

The Machine lingered because the seeds of unity of ethnic groups and racial groups planted by Anton Cermak grew into strong trees. Other machines foundered on the cult of personality—when a strong leader fell, the machine fell apart. This might have happened in Chicago at the end of the Kelly-Nash years but it did not. And that is because of a fellow named Jacob Arvey.

He was a Jew from the old West Side, bright, tough and ambitious, who earned his law degree at the tender age of twenty-one. Arvey knew the language of boardrooms and bordellos. He had street smarts and used them. Because he was one of the first in the Machine to see the natural and profitable link between being a lawyer and being in politics— it was not so obvious in an earlier day—he made money and took power in the Twenty-fourth Ward.

Jack Arvey had been on the fringe of the Irish machine— he knew the Sullivans and the Brennans—but he came into his own when Cermak took over because Cermak had a use for any man who could solidify his power in politics. But Arvey really achieved status with the Kelly-Nash combine: as alderman (and committeeman) of his home ward, he became chairman of the powerful City Council Finance Committee and acted as Kelly's floor manager for all legislation. It was Kelly who took to calling him "Jack" Arvey, while others in the Irish factories pointedly stuck to "Jake" to emphasize Arvey's Jewishness.

Like the cynical George Brennan, Arvey saw Chicago politics as a game that some people played better than others. Jack Arvey played it very well indeed.

"It boils down to work," he said once. "Let me put it in a crude way—put people under obligation to you. Make them your friends. You don't like to hurt a friend. In positions of power in the party, I had to rule against my friends—my close friends. But barring that, I would certainly help a friend. That's politics—put a man under obligation."[2]

Like all successful Machine politicians, Arvey paid attention to details. Broken streets, cracked sidewalks, uncollected garbage, needy neighbors—all the problems in the ward were his problem. "Not a sparrow falls inside the borders of the Twenty-fourth Ward without Arvey's knowing of it. And then, before it hits the ground, there's already a personal history at headquarters, complete to the moment of its tumble," said an admirer.[3]

By the time of the war, Arvey had been committeeman of the Twenty-fourth Ward for eight years and he was only in his forties. He had power because he delivered—his ward would bring in 25,000 Democratic votes at election time and be chagrined if more than a thousand people voted Republican.

Arvey went off to fight in World War II, and he said later that he had no desire to go back into politics when he came back. But he was too good at the game to abandon it, especially because he thought that the Machine would not survive the 1940s, stalemated as it was in the politics of 1931.

Pat Nash was dead and Mayor Ed Kelly was dithering, taking heat daily from the newspapers—especially Marshall Field's new and liberal morning *Sun*. Unfortunately, though, every time Kelly responded and made a bow toward liberal housing for the poor or some other minor reform, he alienated his ethnic constituency.

Arvey resumed control of the Twenty-fourth Ward after his discharge and decided he would stretch his political boundaries. He would become a citywide spokesman of the Jewish cause and, in particular, the Israeli cause. He helped break down the traditional separation between the well-off German Jews of the lakefront Gold Coast and the poorer West Side Jews with their Polish and Russian backgrounds. Because of his new prominence as a Jewish spokesman, he began to move into circles not usually travelled by Machine hacks. He began to meet reformers and learned not to hold his nose when he met them.

Among the odd fish Arvey started to swim with was Paul Douglas, the University of Chicago economics professor who became a reform alderman from Hyde Park in 1939. In the tradition of all Hyde Park reform aldermen, he fought the lonely good fight in City Council.

Douglas was a warm and generous man who was glad to fight for what he saw as right. He had no illusions but he still thought there was such a thing as doing good for humanity in a decent way. (And he was courageous in politics and out of it—when the war came, he enlisted as a marine private at the age of forty-nine and won decorations for his bravery under fire.)

Douglas, unlike many other reformers, had a sense of humor. The City Council was—and still is—a raucous place where physical confrontations were not unknown. Douglas recalled in his memoirs times when Paddy Bauler, often in an advanced state of intoxication during council proceedings, would come up behind his chair and threaten to beat him up. Douglas dared him and Paddy backed down. When Douglas said he was quitting the council to join the Marines and fight in the war, Paddy bawled out, "Good riddance!"

Douglas had an appreciation for these foul-mouthed, utterly cynical and quite savage men who were at the heart of the Machine. He liked to tell a story about the aged Hinky Dink Kenna. Douglas had been speaking about squalid housing conditions in the black ghetto when the old man stood up with a grunt.

"Housing relief! Tain't seemly," he snorted, and clapped his derby on his head and stalked out. It was the last time Hinky Dink went to the Council chamber. A few months later he died, and only a few mourners came to the funeral. Another alderman explained this to Douglas: "If you won't go to other people's funerals, they won't come to yours."[4]

When Jack Arvey eventually lured the learned professor to the Machine without changing any of Douglas's ideologies, Douglas did not feel he was superior to his new colleagues:

"Few of my new associates had ever gone to college," he wrote. "But in terms of innate intelligence, most of them would have held their own with my colleagues on the Midway [at the University of Chicago]. I liked them and believed them better persons than most of the well educated and wealthy utility lawyers who, living in the suburbs, looked down on those they helped to corrupt in the slum areas."[5]

Arvey made a real friend of Douglas and their friendship lasted all their lives. Douglas was fascinated by Arvey:

"He had come up the hard way, from the ghetto, and had made his ward the strongest Democratic center in the nation. . . .

"Arvey was polished, lucid, and conciliatory in manner, but underneath the surface he had a will of steel. His sympathies were basically on the side of the poor, and his acquaintances with the educated Jewish community had given

him an insight into liberal movements that the average politician lacked."[6]

ARVEY SAW THAT THE POSTWAR MACHINE WAS A MESS. THE
organization's much too visible ties to gambling were a lia-
bility: When Kelly, under pressure from the newspapers,
named a new reform police commissioner who declared,
"There'll be no hoodlums or racketeers running around
loose"—the city just laughed.

And the Irish were back to feuding. A roughcut Irishman
named John Duffy had succeeded Arvey as floor leader in
the Council. He was leader of the "Irish turkeys of Beverly,"
a reference to the wealthy Beverly Hills section of the far
Southwest Side. The other major Irish faction was centered
in the working class Bridgeport area.

Duffy was an open bigot. This earned him broad popularity in the ethnic wards because the old Black Belt that ran
through the South Side was splitting its seams, and blacks
were moving into previously all-white neighborhoods. Cot-
tage Grove Avenue, the invisible color line, was breached,
and each time a black family moved onto a new block there
was panic, fear and hatred among whites.

Duffy wanted to use his popularity with the ethnic groups
to take over the Machine. He pushed for the job of chairman
of the Democratic Central Committee, the post held by Kelly.
Kelly was willing to back off from the job—he didn't have the
horses to keep himself in the position—but in a clever move
to block Duffy, he threw support to Jack Arvey. Arvey had
always been a Kelly man; it was therefore better for Arvey to
be in the job than Duffy.

Arvey was suddenly in a position to help put together the
new postwar ticket the Machine would sell to the voters. Kelly

had to go. The newspapers were calling for an end to the regime, and Paul Douglas may have capped it all by threatening to run for mayor himself.

Kelly didn't see it that way at first. He stoutly maintained that though the newspapers were calling him a corrupt hack and a friend of the underworld, no one cared about the papers. Arvey said the voters wouldn't go for him and, to prove it, he had an aide pick some numbers out of the phone book. While Kelly and Arvey listened, the aide told the people who answered the phone that he was making a survey of moviegoing habits—and then he slipped in a question about Kelly.

The *white* voters in the poll didn't like Kelly. They said he had been "too good to the niggers"—what with this public housing business.

Kelly dropped it, then. There were other people who wanted to be mayor. Alderman Duffy certainly regarded himself as the rightful heir, but he wasn't ready to make his move. It would have to be carefully planned—Duffy's reputation was even less attractive than Kelly's to the "newspaper wards" of younger professional people.

Arvey, the Machine hack who worked the precincts and pushed the doorbells and put people under "obligation," decided to experiment with a blue-ribbon candidate to save the organization. As the late Ralph Berkowitz put it: "An old-fashioned Irishman would never have dumped Ed Kelly in 1947. He would have gone down with the ship."[7]

Arvey was not Irish, and he had no intention of sinking. He applied the Cermak lesson to the new situation—a Machine does not stand still, it has to keep moving and reaching out for new groups. It was like a shark: It had to keep moving and eating or it would die.

Arvey called up Martin Kennelly and asked him if he

wanted to run for mayor. Martin Kennelly was a businessman who represented a kind of respectability Arvey thought
the Machine needed. He had been head of the Red Cross. He
looked impressive, with a head of silver hair and classic fea-
tures. A. J. Liebling wrote that he looked like "a bit player
impersonating a benevolent banker"—but to Arvey he looked
like a mayor. Kennelly was the owner of a North Side moving
company who had achieved success the hard way—he had
grown up a poor kid from Bridgeport.

Kennelly was flattered by Arvey's question but uncertain.
He called up a friend, Republican Ralph Berkowitz, and asked
him what he should do. Berkowitz was something of a neutral observer because the Republican party was barely a fac-
tor in Cook County at the time.

Berkowitz told us, "I was surprised by the call. But I thought
it could be a good thing and told him so. Kennelly was no
dummy, I don't care what they say about him now. He read
a lot, he knew things. I told him, what the hell, go ahead.
Some of it worked out all right."[8]

Kennelly agreed to run for mayor for Arvey, even though
he did not like Machine politics. In fact, it can be argued that
he didn't understand Machine politics. His naïveté startled
ordinary Chicagoans. The stunning absurdity of running a
reform candidate as the Machine candidate occurred to everyone, and Jake Arvey's boldness was hailed as nothing short
of genius.

Charles Cleveland, longtime political editor of the old *Chicago Daily News,* recalled, "In his acceptance speech, Kennelly
told the party he didn't believe in spoils politics. It was a
curious sight: The Machine was running a man on a slogan
of 'down with us.' "[9]

Kennelly had been picked in part to combat Kelly's—and
the Machine's—reputation of being easy on the underworld,

but apparently nobody briefed him on his new role. He was asked almost immediately what he intended to do about the crime syndicate in Chicago. "Crime syndicate?" he replied. "I don't know anything about any crime syndicate."[10]

Later in his first term, someone got to Kennelly and convinced him that organized crime really did exist, even in Chicago. Shocked into action by this knowledge, Kennelly announced to the waiting world a plan to combat crime. It was a "Respectability Wave." The amazed Charles Cleveland wrote that Kennelly's plan involved "nothing less than the moral uplift of a city of 3.5 million souls, some of whom haven't noticed any unbearable yearning to be good. The idea is to drive the syndicate out of business the way buggy manufacturers went out of business—for lack of customers. The logic: If everybody obeys the law, then the rackets must starve."[11]

Kennelly's respectability apparently appealed to the voters. With his victory, all those jobs and contracts were saved. Kennelly tried to bring real civil service to Chicago, but his own council blocked him. When he introduced his plan for an independent school board, the aldermen of the Machine were shocked.

The committeemen whose Machine was saved by Kennelly called him "Snow White" behind his back, and Paddy Bauler pinned him as "Fartin' Martin."

A police captain called to testify at a City Council meeting put it this way: "The trouble with Mayor Kennelly is that the only thing he learned in the moving business is never to lift the heavy end."[12]

Was Kennelly that bad? Not really. For example, the crookedness of the Chicago police department was legendary. Lake Shore Drive was so thick with traffic cops looking to shake down motorists caught speeding that one comic got laughs with the line "The Outer Drive is the last outpost of collective bargaining left in the country." Cops also leaned on taverns, brothels and gambling dens for protection money. Kennelly did make changes in the police department and, as Berkowitz said, "The cops couldn't operate as freely as they did before."

"All you read about Kennelly now is he was ineffectual. Well, he was naive, sure, he was naive. He was an honest man." Berkowitz paused when he said this, letting the full weight of the term "honest man" drop in the silence. "But he did a lot of good for the city. A lot of things Daley took credit for later—new streets and public works and all that—that stuff was started by Kennelly. But the committeemen came to hate him and he never got credit."[13]

Jack Arvey would later call Kennelly a mistake, but he was a clever mistake. With Kennelly as the head of city government, all the Machine parts could function. Jobs were kept safe and contracts continued to be greased. Kennelly gave the Machine breathing room for eight years until the far more knowing and skilled Richard Daley came along.

THE SUCCESS OF THE 1947 MAYORAL ELECTION FOR ARVEY WAS more than matched with his successes in 1948. 'Forty-eight was supposed to be the year of the Republican sweep. The Prendergast Machine hack in the White House named Harry Truman was going to be wiped out by Tom Dewey. And Republicans were going to run all over the Democrats in lesser races too. That was the conventional wisdom.

Paul Douglas, back from the war with medals and a wound and his integrity intact, wanted to run for governor. That frightened Arvey and the Machine because the governor of Illinois controlled thousands of patronage jobs and could hold up Chicago schemes proposed in the legislature. The boys knew Douglas from his City Council days; the guy was tough and they couldn't beat up on him. There was no way they would let him run for governor.

Arvey understood that and he made a brilliant move. He shoved Paul Douglas into a run for the U.S. Senate. In the unlikely event that he won, Douglas would make a nice Senator from Illinois. He would be brave and liberal and true, and he would even speak up for Chicago—and he would have nothing to do with controlling patronage.

Still on a "blue ribbon" kick, Arvey now went after Adlai Stevenson II, whose grandfather had been Grover Cleveland's vice president. Stevenson was a wealthy member of Lake Forest high society. He had held some jobs in Washington in the Roosevelt years, including special counsel to the Agricultural Adjustment Administration. During the war, he was assistant to the Navy Secretary Frank Knox, and also worked on plans for the United Nations in London and San Francisco in the last months of the war. Knox, the publisher of the *Chicago Daily News,* died in 1944 and Stevenson came back to Chicago intending to buy the paper. But although he apparently had backers willing to put up enough money to buy it, Stevenson made a low bid and Knox's executors sold the *News* to the more determined John Knight.

Stevenson's jobs as well as his friends gave him a sparkling liberal gloss that Arvey liked very much. Stevenson, however, did not want to be governor. He wanted to go back to Washington as senator, but he let himself be courted.

"It would have been suicidal for Stevenson to have openly sought machine support that spring and summer," according to his official biographer, John Bartlow Martin. "His strength as a candidate—and therefore his value to the machine—lay in his very lack of connection with the machine."[14]

Stevenson held out for the Senate but Arvey was firm about that—no way. Arvey had a difficult juggling act here as party chairman. He had to hold off—and yet satisfy—the cruder committeemen who didn't see the point of dancing with all these goo-goos in the first place. He had to get Paul Douglas out of the way and into Washington where his penchant for real reform would not interfere too much with Machine business. And he needed someone in the governor's chair who could be counted on to go along with the party most of the time. He guessed he could control Stevenson more easily than Douglas.

What made him think that? No one knows and he never told. All Arvey ever said was, "I used to go to bed every night thinking about the ticket.

"The polls showed that President Truman would be beaten badly in 1948. When the head of the ticket is weak, you need a good state ticket.

"I didn't think President Truman could win. But I was sure that Governor (Dwight) Green could be beaten and I thought (Senator Wayland) Brooks could if we got the right man. In 1946, Douglas came to a mass meeting in uniform. He did not make a speech but he waved a greeting to the crowd. I saw his withered hand. Brooks never made a speech without saying, 'I got shrapnel in my back at Château-Thierry and I learned what it means to serve our country.' I knew the shattered hand would dispose of that."[15]

(At the same time, Stevenson would be vulnerable to Brooks because he had not served in the military in the late war—but neither had Govornor Green.)

Stevenson agonized for weeks and months. His Hamlet act was getting on everyone's nerves, including Martin Kennelly's. Kennelly did not take to Stevenson in the first place, and this impressed Stevenson, who overestimated Kennelly's clout in the Machine. Stevenson consulted with his children, with friends and with fellow lawyers.

A longtime Stevenson friend named Dutch Smith recalled that "the night before the decisive meeting, Arvey called me and said he still didn't have an answer and couldn't I do something about it. I went to Adlai's office at nine in the morning and told him, 'If you turn this down, you're not going to have another chance.' He said, 'Can I get Kennelly's support?' I said, 'If you get the nomination he'll have to support you.' "[16] So that afternoon Stevenson finally said yes.

The Arvey experiment worked. The Democratic ticket in that supposed loser of a year carried Illinois by healthy margins. The morning after the election a smiling Harry Truman was holding up the famous "Dewey Defeats Truman" headline in the *Chicago Tribune* for photographers. Paul Douglas was on his way to Washington, and Adlai Stevenson II was heading for Springfield.

Douglas went on to become a respected liberal statesman. He kept close to his Chicago roots and became fast friends with Paddy Bauler, singing "Happy Days Are Here Again" with him in the Deluxe Gardens on campaign trips to the Forty-third Ward through three terms in the Senate.

And Stevenson, who had vacillated so long over the nomination for governor, went on to twice become a presidential candidate whose vacillations became a major political issue. Between the two men, they shaped the destiny of the national party.

JACK ARVEY AND THE CHICAGO MACHINE LOOKED, JUST THEN, like geniuses. Around the country people would point at Douglas and at Stevenson and ask how Machine politics could be so bad if it produced men like these two. The fact that these representatives of the "better elements" had not in any sense been produced by the Machine—had in fact been forced on the Machine by newspaper and reformer pressure and an able political tinkerer willing to take a chance on some new ideas—was obscured in what turned out to be a great public relations coup.

What Arvey did in those few short years in the late 1940s cannot be overestimated. He gave the Machine another thirty years of life. Scholars argued that only a Machine had the strength and the ideological disinterest to elevate such spokesmen for the common good as Stevenson and Douglas. It was a foreshadowing of the affectionate respect the Machine would achieve under Daley for helping to elect John F. Kennedy by a disputed 8,000-vote margin in Illinois in 1960. The liberal conscience of the establishment was always willing to overlook the gritty and crooked nature of a political organization that occasionally did the right thing.

Arvey faded quickly from power when Daley took over the party and the mayor's office between 1953 and 1955. But in his few years as the genius of the Machine, he had done a remarkable thing: he had found a way for the Machine to survive.

12

In Black and White

RACIAL PREJUDICE IS AN INDIVIDUAL MATTER. THE PREJU-diced exist among blacks and whites, Irish and English, Israeli and Arab, wherever cultures, religions and ideas collide among masses of people. Chicago did not invent racial prejudice, but it institutionalized it to an extraordinary degree in its politics, and from this came the eventual downfall of the Machine. Nothing, not even a political machine, lasts forever, but the manner of its death and the aftermath were not inevitable. Today, the politics of race is intensely alive in Chicago, more so than it was thirty years ago. And that is because racial prejudice was woven into the woof of the Machine and city politics.

The first large migration of blacks from the mid-South to Chicago came in the years around World War I. The unskilled jobs in slaughterhouses and on the railroads and in small factories that ringed the downtown district attracted them, along with a freedom of personal life they were denied in Mississippi and Alabama, prime sources of the immigration.

Black people and the ethnics collided in the city, and they fell back into separate neighborhoods like forts. The neighborhoods of Chicago are formed naturally along the branches of the Chicago River, hemmed in by railroad yards and viaducts and sudden outcroppings of sprawling factory complexes. The residents of the city's seventy-eight major neighborhoods (which subdivide into hundreds of small mini-neighborhoods) identified first with the neighborhood (and the local Catholic church), then with the larger city.

People said they came from South Chicago or Pullman or Bridgeport or Canaryville or Hansen Park or Old Town; or, as we have seen, they said they came from Presentation parish or belonged to St. Michael's or came from Seven Holy Martyrs, as though the churches were as fixed as natural geological markers. To an extent, Catholic or not, they still do use these same terms and religious symbols to identify their roots.

Because the neighborhoods are turned in on themselves, they feed on their own prejudices. Chicagoans are part of one of the world's great cities in a sophisticated and—on the surface at least—tolerant world. But in their neighborhoods the wider world view does battle with a studied insularity.

If Poles hated Germans and both hated the Irish, and if the Italians and the Jews warred in the separate neighborhoods of the West Side, they were all united in one common hatred: They despised the blacks.

That hatred spilled into violence in 1919 and it was so revealing that all references to the race riot were largely sealed from public awareness for the next fifty years. Even newspaper reporters in their offices who requested clippings on the riot were automatically referred to a managing editor who was instructed to question the use that would be made of the information.

Race pressures continued long after 1919 was wiped from official memory. Even so, did black people enjoy more freedom than in the South? Yes. Segregation was not what it had been: Blacks worked with whites, were recruited for the police force, published newspapers, played in politics, ate in whatever restaurants they could afford, did not have "separate but equal" drinking fountains or schools. But at night, a black man went home to his own neighborhood, down in the "Black Belt" on the South Side. The Belt stretched south from the old whorehouse Levee district along the spine of State Street and east of it. It was about six square miles and it barely increased in size from the end of World War I until 1950, although its population went from 109,595 in 1920 to 492,265 in 1950. The human beings whose presence is told by those numbers had nowhere to live except on top of each other.[1]

Gradually the black pioneer society grew into its own kind of sophistication. It grew rich and somewhat prejudiced itself, toward a larger, rural-born and uneducated later-arriving population. There were tensions between these groups and a prejudice as basic as skin color was common. One old-timer remembers lighter-skinned blacks forming their own cliques as members of an unofficial "blue vein" club for those so light-skinned that they could see their veins under the skin.

The Machine, though it was in a position to deal with it,

was paralyzed by the race problem and, particularly, by the black housing problem. The practical politician knows that nothing lasts forever. He only wants it to last his time and to his advantage. This limited policy kept the Machine from addressing the housing problem for too long.

The blacks wanted out of their ghetto. But how could the Machine encourage this without breaking up the old ethnic neighborhoods that gave it its strength? Nor did black Machine leaders have any interest in breaking up the tight black ghetto. Under Bill Dawson it was a powerful force as well as economically tied to the Dawson machine. Why let the chickens get out of the coop?

There was a white conscience in the city, but it had largely abdicated political power to the Machine. Businessmen dealt with the Machine on a businesslike basis; if things worked well, they made money and kept their mouths shut. Since the city's politics had been based for so long on deals and jobs and contracts, there was no traditional way of handling the kind of ideological issue that black-white relations were quickly becoming. Inside the Democratic party, Roosevelt liberals were unwilling to attack the Machine for its racial policies; after all, the Chicago Machine was an important prop for the Democrats and their liberal stance in national politics.

Marshall Field III was an exception. The grandson of the wily old merchant who had pioneered the idea of the department store, Field made housing for blacks one of his key issues when he started the liberal morning *Sun* to go head-to-head against Colonel Robert McCormick's reactionary *Tribune* in 1941.

When educated whites did protest the city's growing racism, lower-class whites felt embattled on every side. They bitterly resented getting advice on brotherhood from people who were buying their way out of the city's racial troubles by moving to posh suburbs or restricted neighborhoods. Immigrant groups like the Bohemians and Poles traditionally put all their money in their homes. Block-busting techniques by real estate developers who saw big profits in turning over white areas on the edge of the ghetto threatened their only assets.

And so along with the racial division, the bitterness between the working-class Machine constituency and the upper-middle-class whites drawn to reform politics grew. It was clear to white Machine politicians, and most Machine blacks, that there could be no mixing of the races—not in this life, not in Chicago. When blacks attempted to move out of the ghetto, violence met them in a series of incidents that flare across the city's history.

There was some black housing built by the federal government in the late 1930s, including the pioneer low-rise housing project called Ida B. Wells Homes in 1937. But when Ed Kelly, as part of his wooing of the Dawson Republicans, endorsed limited public housing, he got into trouble with the white ethnic communities for it.

The Second World War cracked the issue. Just too many people from the black rural South came to Chicago in a rush; the problem could not be ignored. (The Illinois Central line gave the train called *The City of New Orleans* a new nickname: "The Fried Chicken Special," because everyone packed a box lunch for the journey.)

Black realtor Dempsey Travis recalled his own efforts to build up a business selling blacks property in white areas during the early 1950s: "I got to be very good at matching South Side people with West Side housing. Many blacks chose Douglas Park because the West Side Jewish residents being displaced by black South Side immigrants never reacted violently, as did the Irish and Poles on the Southeast and Southwest sides. The Jewish homeowners in Douglas Park were so cordial to me that I would sometimes get up enough nerve to ask them why they were moving.

" 'We're moving west to California,' they always said. I thought it was strange that so many people from the same area would be moving to the West Coast. Later on, a Jewish friend told me that 'California' was synonymous for Skokie, Illinois.' " (Skokie, a north suburb, is almost totally Jewish today.)[2]

The issue of race, then, infected most real estate transactions in the city from the beginning of the Second World War to the condo developments and conversion in the early 1970s, to the larger and more peaceful influx of Puerto Ricans and, more important, Mexicans into the city.

At the heart of the story of what happened to public housing Chicago-style is a remarkable woman named Elizabeth Wood, who came to the city from southern Illinois, where she had studied with her biologist and former missionary father at Illinois Wesleyan. Though she had taught poetry at Vassar briefly and once published a now-out-of-print novel, she became a social worker, continuing the pioneer tradition of Chicagoan Jane Addams, who had started the world's first neighborhood settlement house.

Miss Wood was smart and hard-working, and she knew what she was talking about. Fearless in bad neighborhoods, she worked for good with a practical skill and an unblinking knowledge of how bad Chicago could really be.

Eventually she moved on to the Metropolitan Housing Board and the state Housing Board and turned her interests toward giving shelter to the poor and clearing the slums of the city. In 1938, Mayor Kelly named her executive secretary of the new Chicago Housing Authority which was to oversee the "study" of public housing and how it might apply to the city.

A man named Milton Shufro was the CHA public relations man and he acted as go-between for Wood and Kelly. City Hall regulars who were around then remember that Shufro could get almost instant access to Kelly, and that some of the old-timers resented it.

Shufro said that after a time, "Negro organizations, labor organizations, civic and church organizations became the core of our support. We became symbols. This became true not through any particular magic, but due to the fact that our program and administration was good in the sense of being decent and honest, just and fair."[3]

That kind of program would give a committeeman goosebumps, but the pressure was building on Kelly for public housing. Marshall Field III was even putting up his own funds to help start a private low-cost housing development on Sedgwick Street on the North Side (it is still there and is still good housing).

Public housing was hot as an issue because of race, but there was more—it was a classic confrontation between liberal and conservative approaches to government and, in Chicago, between the neighborhoods and the do-gooders on the lakefront.

Liberal Elmer Gertz, an attorney who championed public housing, said it was more than shelter for the poor that was the issue, but "visible proof that this is a country which believes in the dignity of all human beings."[4]

That was not the language of the Machine, yet it did not matter much as long as public housing remained a nice reform issue, under study, but providing no threat of immediate and drastic action.

By war's end, Miss Wood's little empire supervised nearly

eight thousand family units in ten projects scattered over the city. They were humanely run units where people lived in dignity. They were desegregated for the most part because that was the way Elizabeth Wood saw things—at a time when the official policy of the National Association of Real Estate Boards was openly racist, saying realtors should keep minorities out of new neighborhoods.

The federal government went along with this segregated housing idea. The Federal Housing Administration and the Home Loan Bank Board issued directives on how "inharmonious groups" should be kept out of new neighborhoods. Housing expert Charles Abrams remarked, "The official manual of the FHA during this period reads like a chapter from Hitler's Nuremberg laws."[5]

Wood moved carefully and courageously around these neighborhood and official prejudices. She felt that a system of racial quotas in public housing would keep the idea of integrated public housing alive. As late as 1955 she said, "It is as sure as the spring follows winter that in due time, the city of Chicago will be a city of unsegregated neighborhoods, an unsegregated city."

Though Chicago in the 1980s has been called America's most segregated city, she has been proven right in vast areas of the North Side where neighborhoods have been integrated and stabilized by the condo development laws introduced in 1972. Owners of apartments in large buildings may be black or white—as long as they meet the mortgage payments, they are owners.

Ironically, what happened to public housing in Chicago is one reason that segregation is still so entrenched in large areas of the South, Southwest, West and Northwest Sides of the city. Mention public housing and blacks—and whites—cringe. The image of the CHA today is not of new and shining cities of integration but of payoffs, scandals, projects run by gangs, urine-stained corridors, broken elevators and casual everyday murder. Concentration of the poor in inhuman-scale public housing has allowed real estate men to grow rich at public expense.

It started with better intentions, particularly with the Wells Homes on the South Side and the Cabrini homes on the near North Side. The first part of the Cabrini project was started by CHA in 1942. Cabrini was named for the first American-born saint, Mother Frances Cabrini, who worked for the poor in Chicago. A labor leader's name was tacked on later, when the project grew, and it is now officially called Cabrini-Green.

The project was located west of Old Town in a largely Italian neighborhood called Little Hell. When Mayor Kelly broke ground he said, "These homes, built by the Chicago Housing Authority, symbolize the Chicago that is to be. We cannot continue as a nation half slum and half palace."

Seventy-five percent of the first 586 families who moved in were white and 25 percent were black. The small, neat, plain units were a big improvement over the tenement flats without toilet facilities and with dirt floors the tenants left behind. As late as 1949, a CHA survey would claim there were 1,178,000 families in Chicago—and only 906,000 "standard" dwelling units, fit for human habitation.

On July 8, 1949, Congress passed a public housing act, partly because of the pressure for housing created by returning servicemen intent on raising big families. On that same day, Elizabeth Wood's CHA proposed a big and bold plan for housing to Mayor Kennelly. The federal money was waiting, and Wood wanted to build forty thousand low-rent housing units over a six-year period, taking $500 million of federal monies to do the job.

Could Chicago pass up that much money?

At the same time, New York City decided it could not, and built all the public housing and took all the public money it could get.

Los Angeles, at the same time, debated the idea, started a plan and then, a year later, backed out and lost the money already invested.

Detroit saw a huge project started—and then cut back when a public housing opponent was elected mayor.

Everyone, more or less, saw the need for public housing and slum clearance. But the question nagged: When the slums were torn down, where would the slum dwellers go to live while housing was being built? And where would the new public housing be built—on vacant land sites in the outlying (white) areas of the city or on the cleared slum land in places like the Black Belt?

Wood's CHA had considered the problems and picked the sites she wanted to begin with. There were 15 in slum areas for a planned 10,400 dwelling units. Another 2,112 units were to go on vacant land in white areas. That was the plan she sent to City Hall.

And all hell broke loose.

JOHN DUFFY, THE "TURKEY IRISHMAN" OF JAKE ARVEY'S DESCRIPtion, hated the idea of public housing, and he led the fight in the City Council against it. Only seven aldermen stood with Miss Wood for the plan. The forty-three who were against it voted for a subcommittee of aldermen to make its own site selection. Duffy fumed about the CHA and its supposed plans to override the great good sense of the City Council. Duffy said they were all communists at the CHA anyway or at least "a little tinted."

The subcommittee was headed by Emil V. Pacini, a public

housing foe from the neglected steel mill neighborhood on
the far Southeast Side. Would the subcommittee select its
sites by poring over the figures supplied by all the CHA's
surveys and studies? Of course not. Then how? By touring
the city and picking out their own sites.

On a sunny day in March, the aldermen of the subcommittee boarded a bus outside City Hall. It was a hilarious
outing. The boys were in a good mood. On their way to check
out a list of possibilities, they pointed out a notorious brothel
and speculated about ways the committeemen of the wards
they passed through might increase their bank accounts. Reporters were amused.

On subsequent days, when CHA supporters Aldermen
Robert Merriam and Ben Becker were on the bus, the others
spent their time razzing the two reformers. Neither of them
was good at taking a joke: Merriam was a stiff, formal
product of the University of Chicago milieu, and Becker was
on the lookout for any remark that could be thought anti-
Semitic.

The joke was supposed to be that the aldermen were out to
"get" the CHA and those who supported it: They would
select impossible sites located as punishment in the wards of
the traitors Merriam and Becker. Only it was not a joke.

The aldermen trooped back to City Hall and met in a
closed session that lasted past midnight. Outlandish propos-
als were moved and seconded. One Machine stalwart, P. J.
(Parky) Cullerton, had to intervene to prevent a project being located on the University of Chicago tennis courts—as
punishment for Merriam. Cullerton was no public houser,
but he could see that the newspapers were not laughing.

A "compromise plan" was worked out, but the number of
units to be built on vacant sites—which meant in white areas—was small. The deal had been cut: Public housing was

not to be used to integrate the city of Chicago. Instead, it would be used to warehouse black families inside the slum neighborhoods they had always occupied. And because the land the Housing Authority would be allowed to build on was so small, there would be no alternative to massive high-rise developments.

Elizabeth Wood and her CHA put a bright face on the City Council's work and said there was nothing wrong with the idea of high rises. There would be more open space for children to play in. They talked about grand concepts and bold design. Maybe Wood believed it or maybe she was merely going along with what had to be.

The great "compromise" plan did punish the enemies of the antihousing faction that dominated the Machine. Two of the vacant land sites would be in Ben Becker's ward, "bus window" selections chosen by "the boys" during those hilarious rides in March.

Becker went to Duffy to protest. "John, you damned fool," he said. "You're running for president of the County Board. Not one Jew will vote for you."

Duffy sneered to Becker, "The trouble with you Jews is, when you get backed against the wall, you start crying. When we Irish were backed against the wall by the Ku Klux Klan we used clubs, we used bricks, we used stones. But what do you Jews do? You don't fight. You start crying. Well, you asked for it and you're going to get it."[6]

This brutal attitude prevailed in the brutal game of public housing. Slablike monoliths started rising in the black slums and families were crammed inside.

Wood said, "I was so undercut politically that I was feeble, I was floundering around. We no longer had power to select where the projects were going to go, and we had very little space to work with, so we had to go to the high rises . . . . It seemed to me so antifamily and inhumane but it was just an inevitable flow because land acquisition was so difficult."[7]

The dream of integrated public housing failed as well. There had been troubles before: a low-rise project near Midway Airport in 1946 prompted a white neighborhood riot when blacks moved in; blacks were attacked in Englewood, Park Manor and Trumbull Park in 1949 for the same reasons. But the Trumbull Park riot in 1953 on the far South Side sealed the fate of the reform plan to make public housing work.

Sticking to her tattered quota system, Wood allowed a mailman named Donald Howard, twenty-four, to move his family into the all-white housing project. Three more black families followed. By the time the moving vans showed up, the neighborhood was ripe with tomatoes and rocks to use as missiles. Young white men with powder bombs were arrested. It took 700 policemen finally to restore peace to the project.

The aldermen were furious. Not with the whites, of course, but with Elizabeth Wood for allowing blacks to move into a white housing project.

One alderman said, "There's vindictiveness and revenge in this picture because we have pinkoes in the CHA."[8]

Trumbull Park was the last white housing project, and 1954 was the last year on the job for Wood. She had failed but she did not resign without protest. During her last months in office she fought paper wars to stop the aldermen from gutting her agency.

On TV in 1954, Wood said the Machine was racist. "The truth is that the differences which have arisen between the commissioners and the executive secretary have been related primarily to the issue of the elimination of segregation in housing.

"This policy, which I have personally always believed to be

a basic and unavoidable principle of democracy, was not of my making, but is rooted in the laws of the state of Illinois, the resolution of the city council, and the state policies of the authority. . . ."9

Within hours, the CHA board, dominated by the Council, fired her after sixteen years as secretary.

The tragedy of public housing in Chicago still festers. Enraged tenants crammed in substandard high rises—often without elevator service or even water during freezing winters—have denounced the black management of the CHA under Mayor Washington as they denounced the old white management. Nothing is done; neglect is the order of the day in CHA ranks. The human tragedy continues and only becomes worse because there is no money now to correct the mistakes of the past and no inclination to move toward a system of making private housing more available to the poor.

A year after Elizabeth Wood resigned, the new mayor of the city, Richard J. Daley, broke ground for new high rises to vastly expand the renamed Cabrini-Green project (linking the names of a saint and a labor leader). Even before it was finished in 1962, Cabrini-Green became the symbol of everything bad about the projects in Chicago.

Because the design of the buildings is poor, elevators are located on the outside of the building walls, making them largely ineffectual during the usual severe winter. Because the halls are dangerous and ruled by gangs, garbage disposal is simplified: garbage is thrown out the windows. When workmen repair brick work on scaffolds outside the buildings, they are subject to teasing sniper fire from the inmates of these hells. Preschool children play more often on the catwalks high above the city streets than in the dangerous "open areas" on ground level.

The rage of black people who were kept concentrated in

overcrowded ghettoes built. The seeds of future riots were sown and also the seeds of the Machine's self-destruction. Perhaps people like Duffy and Cullerton understood that in their day and merely ignored the future for the profit of the present, or perhaps they did not. Their legacy to the city is an awful one.

Elizabeth Wood is still alive. Some years after her ouster, she was succeeded by Charles (Chuckie) Swibel, a West Side flophouse landlord who became one of the Machine's "fixit" boys under Daley and, still later, a close pal of Jane Byrne. In the Machine tradition, he did public service even as he privately became rich in the process.

His successor, under Mayor Washington, was Renault Robinson, a former cop and self-styled civil rights advocate who ruled the CHA so ineptly from the first that Washington was forced to replace him after a few months.

The faces have changed inside CHA but the legacy of misery remains.

CHICAGO HISTORICAL SOCIETY

Carter Harrison I

Carter Harrison II

CHICAGO HISTORICAL SOCIETY

CHICAGO HISTORICAL SOCIETY

CHICAGO TRIBUNE PHOTO

Cartoon showing the madams, pimps, gamblers and conmen of Bathhouse John Coughlin's first ward.

(Below left) Michael (Hinky Dink) Kenna and Bathhouse John Coughlin at the 1924 Democratic Convention.

(Above) Mayor William (Big Bill) Thompson at a city council meeting with cowgirl Frankie Gibson, cowboy Buck Spencer and an unidentified Indian holding Spencer's horse.

The founder of the Machine, Anton Cermak, during his 1931 campaign for mayor.

(Right) Alderman Mathias (Paddy) Bauler on his retirement from the city council.

UPI/THE BETTMANN ARCHIVE

Rep. William Dawson conferring with Alderman-elect
Ralph Metcalfe.

CHICAGO TRIBUNE PHOTO

CHICAGO TRIBUNE PHOTO

Jacob (Jack) Arvey on his way
to Lyndon Johnson's 1965
inaugural.

UPI/BETTMANN NEWSPHOTOS

War protesters and Chicago police outside the Hilton
Hotel during the 1968 convention.

First-term mayor Daley and Adlai Stevenson II greet
former President Harry Truman.

UPI/BETTMANN NEWSPHOTOS

AP/WIDE WORLD PHOTOS

Mayor Richard J. Daley of Chicago shouts at Senator Abraham Ribicoff of Connecticut during the latter's speech nominating George S. McGovern for president in 1968.

AP/WIDE WORLD PHOTOS

Mayor Michael Bilandic wipes a tear at his farewell speech in 1979.

Jane Byrne announces her candidacy in 1985.

UPI/BETTMANN NEWSPHOTOS

Harold Washington and Richard M. Daley, the late mayor's son, during one of the TV debates in 1983.

13
Daley

JACK ARVEY SHOWED THAT THE MACHINE HAD TO ACCEPT change in order to survive. What happened to public housing showed that reform, when pressed upon the Machine by outside influences, could be twisted beyond all recognition. The basic Machine dilemma remained: Change must happen, but it must be the kind of change that would not threaten the central structure of the Machine coalition.

From the end of World War II, "reform" came to mean only one thing in Chicago—a full voice for blacks in local government. The city was racially polarized, and the Machine supported and profited from this polarization. This could not change.

The leaders of the Machine may not have understood this at first. The Machine did not lack talent and foresight of a kind, as Arvey had shown. But its leaders' perceptions were often impaired by the long history and the long success of Machine government in Chicago. Back in the fat days of the fifties, the city was still making money for the boys who met in the old Morrison Hotel to decide who was going to run things into the 1960s. If there were those like Arvey who saw that long-term structural changes were going to have to come, they contented themselves with small forays into reform for the moment.

Because he was a Jew from the West Side, Jack Arvey wasn't ever going to be mayor of Chicago, even if that was what he wanted. He had been pushed to the front of the Machine to dress it up, but he had used the job to take power from John Duffy and his boisterous crowd of lace-curtain Irish from Beverly. Because Arvey was supposed to front but not necessarily to win, the victories of Kennelly, Stevenson and Douglas in the two golden years of 1947 and 1948 gave him more power than he had hoped for. He was now in a position to be king maker, if not king.

Of the three cards in hand, the only problem was with Stevenson. Stevenson wanted no part of the gritty of Chicago Machine politics; he suffered the Machine because it was necessary but he had his eye on the Main Chance, and for him that was in Washington.

Did Stevenson agree to let Arvey be in charge of patronage if he was elected governor? Not at all. He didn't have to. He had thirty thousand or so patronage jobs and he didn't know that many people. Arvey, via the Machine, had a system for filling jobs. Arvey told Stevenson he would not interfere on major appointments but "as to the rank and file, you'll have to get help somewhere—you don't know enough people to fill all the jobs—and if you need help, I'll give it to you."[1]

Like his son after him, Stevenson had a manner that made downstate pols complain that he talked down to them—and never picked up a check. As a result, Jake Arvey assigned Michael Howlett to teach Adlai the ropes. But Stevenson disliked Howlett's gravel voice, boisterous manner and cynical clowning. Howlett was replaced as the Machine's liaison with Stevenson by a Bridgeport stalwart named Richard J. Daley.

Daley worked out. Arvey wanted him to be state revenue director, and Stevenson agreed. He liked Daley's dull and plodding style; he needed a detail man.

Richard J. Daley was born in Bridgeport's Eleventh Ward, where the Irish had first settled in Chicago. He was an only child whose mother was a schoolteacher of strict standards; she lavished affection on him and helped him with his schoolwork. Bridgeport was the world to Daley. He never outgrew his pride in the place or his Bridgeport accent, the equivalent of the speech that prevails in Queens or South Philadelphia. In later years, some would imagine that they could gauge Daley's intelligence by the roughness of his speech. These people made a very grave error.

Daley learned ambition and determination from his mother. He was not quick or brilliant, but brilliance counted for little in hardscrabble, working-class Bridgeport. Daley put himself through law school at night at DePaul University, and it was no picnic. Some of the posh lawyers of Chicago's business elite had a tendency to sneer at Daley's background of night-school drudgery. This, again, was a mistake.

Daley had an affection for numbers and detail that won him grudging respect. He seemed part of a new political wave of detached professionals minding the business of government. In fact, he was not: He was of the old breed, the Cermak breed. Like Cermak, he rose to prominence on negative virtues. He hung onto dull but important jobs; he liked numbers and kept them in orderly columns: numbers of jobs, of tax dollars, of deposits and contracts, of votes, the numbers that are at the root of the Machine and of politics.

Daley's hard work sometimes made him the butt of his fellow legislators' jokes. Then and now, Springfield is a singularly dull city. A number of legislators have always found ways to liven things up; their sex parties and drinking bouts are the stuff of legend. Scandal never attached to Daley; he spent his Springfield nights writing long and earnest letters of love home to his wife Eleanor (Sis) in Chicago.

Milburn Peter Akers, political editor of the *Sun,* wrote that Daley then "was the best exhibit of the hardworking, decent, honest organization politician that the Kelly machine can produce."[2]

It was an estimate shared by Jack Arvey, who had big things in mind for Dick Daley.

ARVEY'S REPUTATION AS A GENIUS COLLAPSED ABRUPTLY IN 1950 when he made the mistake of slating Police Captain Daniel Gilbert as candidate for Cook County sheriff. Gilbert was known as the World's Richest Cop because of the fortune he had accumulated while a policeman from illegal gambling operations. Both Adlai Stevenson and Paul Douglas recoiled from Arvey because of his decision to slate Gilbert.

Senator Estes Kefauver brought his Senate Committee to Investigate Organized Crime to the hometown of organized crime for a little show that summer. He did not think to ask Dan Gilbert to testify before his committee and Gilbert felt slighted. He volunteered to testify—and in public—while in the middle of his campaign for sheriff.

Arvey was appalled. "Obviously, I blundered. I had made a mistake," he said later. "Actually, I thought a police captain with Dan Gilbert's wide experience would have made a fine sheriff—worlds better than the man who defeated him. But of course . . . when he insisted on going over to Kefauver to testify, voluntarily, and I pleaded with him not to go—I knew that there was going to be trouble."[3]

Gilbert not only made trouble, he was hilarious. He told the stunned committee of his wealth, of his securities worth $360,000 and of the $45,000 in income he had reported on his last IRS return. He babbled on and on mostly about his prowess as a gambler. "I have been a gambler at heart all my life."

Rudolph Halley, chief committee counsel, found voice to ask, "This gambling you do, that is not legal gambling, is it?"

Gilbert seemed struck by the thought and paused. "Well, no." He paused again. "No, it is not legal. No."[4]

Kefauver had no intention of making Gilbert's testimony public but *Chicago Sun-Times* reporter Ray Brennan found the printer who was to set the testimony in type for the committee and conned him into giving him a set of proof sheets. The story of the World's Richest Cop hit the front pages five days before the election.

Gilbert went down, of course, but he dragged the whole ticket with him, including Senator Scott Lucas, Democratic Majority leader in the U.S. Senate, who lost to the obscure downstate Republican, Everett M. Dirksen.

One of the few winners in that year—he had been endorsed by Stevenson and Douglas—was Richard Daley, who won the county clerk's job by a margin of 147,000 votes. It was an important win because of all the losers falling around him.

The Machine was in temporary shambles and the blame was on Arvey. He resigned as chairman of the party in 1950, and old Joe Gill of the Forty-ninth Ward on the North Side was put in as temporary chairman until the next election, in 1953. Arvey was allowed to stay on as delegate from the Machine to the national committee, and he helped them to select Stevenson as the Democratic sacrificial lamb of 1952 against Eisenhower.

The maneuvering began to replace Gill and take over the Machine. John Duffy, who had lost the race for president of the County Board, his pal Clarence Wagner and Judge James McDermott were the old-line "turkey Irish" boys. They were arrayed against the Bridgeporters led by Richard Daley, who wanted to be chairman of the party.

The deal wasn't complicated. Wagner was committeeman of Canaryville, the Fourteenth Ward. He would resign his job in such a way as to push McDermott into it just in time to be elected chief committeeman and chairman of the party.

Daley had his friends as well but he had more: God was on his side. Shortly before the election, while speeding off in his city-owned limousine to a fishing trip in Canada, Wagner went off the road, crashed and was killed. Everyone on the Duffy side mourned; it was no longer possible to stop Daley.

Gill was for Daley and so were old-timers like Paddy Bauler and Charlie Weber. They might have had personal reasons not to back McDermott, now that Wagner was dead.

Long after the matter, in the comfort of his beloved De-Luxe Gardens saloon, Bauler told a reporter that the death of Clarence Wagner came as a financial blow to him and others. "You could trust the guy (Wagner). Only . . . we had this pot, see? And certain things that we got together on and voted for went into the pot, cuttin' it up at the end of the year—the guys who were in, that is. So Clarence has this envelope (in a safety deposit box) and then he gets kilt and that son of a bitch McDermott sits there pretty as pie and won't give back our money."[5]

McDermott said he had taken the envelope to make sure the money went to Wagner's widow.

What kind of money? Paddy said, "It was a hundred grand."

It came from various deals common in the hall of power—from franchise renewals with places like the phone company or gas company. As Weber put it: "They wanted one of them exceptions to the ordinance or some bullshit like that. So they pay and we give them what they want."

Bauler said, "Listen, you think we should do things for them people for nothin'? They got to have somethin' done—raise the cab fare or get a city parkin' lot lease or somethin' like that—holy Cry, you don't think they expect to get it for nothin', do you? What's fair is fair, you know."[6]

Daley was elected chairman of the eighty-member central committee in 1953. Two years later, he would combine the power of the chair—the system of the "committeeman's letter" and control of patronage jobs set up by Sullivan and Brennan—with the power of the jobs controlled by the Mayor's office.

As Bauler put it, "He was the dog with the big nuts"[7] now and everyone was amazed, wondering—who the hell is this dullard from Bridgeport suddenly sitting at the pinnacle of the old Machine?

14

Brothers' Boy

FOR CHICAGO, A RELATIVELY NEW CITY, BRIDGEPORT, WHERE
Daley grew up, is an old neighborhood. There are a few
good restaurants on Halsted Street and the famous old
Schaller's Pump Saloon, which has been open for more than
a century—including during Prohibition. The saloon is right
across the street from the headquarters of the Eleventh Ward.
Narrow in shape, the neighborhood is also narrow in its attitudes and its closed environment. People are fixed in their
loyalty to their family and their church. Their attitudes about
race are fixed as well.

Daley went to De LaSalle High School down on 35th Street
in a neighborhood that was part of the Black Belt. Dever,

Kelly, Kennelly and Bilandic—all mayors in their time—had attended this high school. The Christian Brothers, then and now, run a tough school, long on discipline. Daley, like the others, was a Brothers' Boy, and that marked him.

The school taught Irish kids to put on a good face for the world and polish their shoes every morning. Daley said he learned to wear an ironed shirt and clean suit there and to face the world smiling.

As a youth, he was a member of the Hamburger Social and Athletic Club in the neighborhood and Mike Royko has suggested that he (with his club members) was a participant in the 1919 race riots—but there is no evidence of this.

Daley learned shorthand and how to type at De LaSalle, and he used those skills to become a secretary to the pols in the Kelly-Nash Machine. He served his time in the ward office in Springfield in county government. He moved up the ranks very slowly, almost glacially. But all that changed in 1953, when he captured the chairmanship. Then all the caution, all the diffidence seemed to fall away.

Arvey had advised him not to take the job as chairman because it smelled too much of "bossism" and would hurt Daley if he wanted to run for mayor—which he did. But Daley brushed the more cautious older man's advice aside. He saw the beauty of it—having control of city and party in his hands alone. He saw the uses of power, and he reached for power with a sure instinct.

It was clear that the Machine intended to dump Kennelly in 1955. Eight years of goo-goo government had thoroughly sickened the Morrison Hotel crowd. Bill Dawson was mad at Kennelly for interfering with the gambling operations in his black wards, and others had other beefs—primarily about jobs. The dumbbell had put twelve thousand perfectly good patronage jobs under civil service. Why? Because it was the right thing to do. How could you trust a guy like that? You couldn't predict what he'd decide was the right thing to do next. The mope was already rich, and he didn't do things for money. Nobody in politics could understand him. He had to go before he did more harm to the Machine.

In the closed nomination meeting inside the truly smoke-filled party headquarters in the Morrison Hotel on Madison Street in the Loop, fifty committeemen of the city weighed Daley and Kennelly. Kennelly got one vote. Daley got forty-nine.

But Kennelly didn't get the message. He decided to fight the Machine in the primary. He portrayed Daley, who had had good press in the past for his work in Springfield and the county, as the dupe of evil men in the Machine. He said Daley was gullible. The papers took up the line. The *Tribune* summed up:

"Mr. Daley is no hoodlum, but if he runs he will be the candidate of the hoodlum element. He will also be the candidate of those who wish to load the city's offices once again with political payrollers and thus undo the great work of Mayor Kennelly in giving the City a real merit system of appointments and promotions. Mr. Daley will also be the candidate of those who want to see the city purchase of supplies and contracts let in the good old-fashioned way, with a nice percentage for the politicians."

God, Daley hated the press. He saw reporters as smart-aleck elitists who didn't understand a damned thing about the way politics really worked. In his primary campaign, his theme was simple:

"My opponent says, 'I took the politics out of the schools, I took the politics out of this and I took the politics out of that.' I say to you: There's nothing wrong with politics. Good politics is good government."[1]

The line became a catch phrase of his administration. It underlines a point debated today, and not just in Chicago: There are evils in an impersonal, bureaucratic government which is not accountable to the voters, just as there are evils in patronage. Which is worse?

Big Bill Dawson, the black giant of Chicago politics, won the election for Daley. Daley swept the city's black wards and the so-called river wards along the branches of the Chicago River where the old, entrenched ethnic ways still prevail, where a job is still a job and where the underworld still weighs in heavily.

The rest of white Chicago was divided, but the Machine's "Solid Eleven" wards produced the votes for victory. Kennelly sighed on election night, "They're unbeatable, just unbeatable, aren't they?"[2]

The Solid Eleven went on to give the Daley people victory in the April general election when the Republicans put up a strong goo-goo named Robert Merriam, the Hyde Park reform voice just as his father, Charles, had been in the Sullivan and Brennan days.

It was a wonderful night of victory for the boys. The beer halls were filled with shouting and laughing men. Paddy Bauler, donning a green top hat, danced a jig in his saloon for Daley and utttered his most memorable cry: "Chicago ain't ready for reform yet!"[3]

DALEY MOVED SWIFTLY TO UNDO THE DAMAGE CAUSED BY Kennelly's civil service. He fired liberal lawyer Steve Hurley as civil service boss and put in someone he thought he could trust. William A. Lee was the frail, soft-spoken head of the Bakery Drivers' Union as well as chairman of the joint council in Chicago of the AFL. From Daley's point of view—and the view of organized labor in Chicago, particularly the powerful building trades—it was a great choice.

Bill Lee called the shots on every labor move in City Hall for the next thirty years, a period of incredible labor peace. While other cities saw public employee strikes, Chicago had no such problems until long after Daley's death. And the police and fire departments remained nonunion through Daley's reign and beyond.

Lee and the building trades worked a quid pro quo with the city. City patronage jobs in the trades—the carpenters and plumbers and other assorted loafers who fixed the pipes at City Hall—were paid "the prevailing rate" of wages. Thus, they were more equal than their counterparts in private industry where building layoffs and weather delays were frequent. The city worker in the trades paid his union dues, made political kickbacks and still came out ahead. His high hourly rate was paid day in and day out, regardless of the work; the guy in the private sector never could do as well. Labor formed a cozy relationship with Daley and the Machine because Daley gave them a core of money to buy labor peace.

Lee was never colorful in the manner of, say, the old head of the plumber's union, Umbrella Mike Boyle who was said to hang a partially open umbrella upside down when he visited his favorite saloon to collect political payoffs in.

It didn't matter. Politics was about money, jobs and business, and the colorful old days of the Hinky Dinks, Sullivans, even the day of Paddy Bauler was passing.

It was difficult a decade after his death for Chicagoans to have a good perspective on Richard J. Daley. He was mayor for twenty-one years and two months. He was larger than life both as a symbol of the city and the Machine and in person. When Daley walked into a room, the band struck up "Chi-

cago, That Toddlin' Town!" and the spotlight found him
and moved to the podium in a din of applause. He carried it
off with some humor and an odd shyness. He seemed to be
drawn in bright colors like a cartoon while the world around
him was in weak blacks and grays.

Daley was imitated by comedians, his mangled syntax was
celebrated by friends and foes, every detail of his workday
was gone over again and again. He assumed office in 1955
but not the airs of office. Once, as mayor, he went to meet a
top businessman at the exclusive Tavern Club. He arrived
early, and his host was not yet there. Daley waited with other
nonmembers in the foyer—until a shocked club official recognized him and brought him immediately to a table.

Daley went to Mass every morning at his neighborhood
church before the work day began. What did he pray for?

He went home every night to the same Bridgeport bungalow he lived in all his life. Why was he content with such
humble surroundings?

Daley was a gentleman until he felt himself pushed into the
pose of a streetfighter. Unlike ethnic leaders in other cities in
his time, he never presented or allowed a public pose of
racism or ethnic prejudice. He went into black wards and
white ones for their ward affairs. He ate pigs' knuckles and
collard greens when he had to and bagels and blood sausage
and pasta, and he could even dance the Polish polkas on his
surprisingly small feet.

This short, portly man with the earnest manner and the
inability, ever, to express all he had to say in good English,
was more than a popular politician. He *was* Chicago in a way
that was so overwhelming that it shaped and limited all opponents and all opposition. This peculiar identification of a
city with a Machine hack who lacked grace of manner or
person infuriated his foes. Republican strategist Ralph

Berkowitz, a Daley contemporary, insisted that Daley's appeal was a fluke, that the man himself was "a nothing."

"If a lot of guys he was waiting around for hadn't died at the right time, he never would have gone anywhere," Berkowitz said. "And all that stuff about Irish loyalty, how everybody in the Machine loves Daley and always loved him? They didn't love Daley. Daley was just another guy who could deliver for them. Daley got elected, he gave people jobs, they got to make money. That was what these newspaper guys like to call love."[4]

Daley was fifty-three years old when he became mayor. He was seasoned in the ways of ward politics, of high-level infighting, of legislative maneuvering. He knew exactly what he wanted to do with this Machine. He did it all and it became his. This is the way he worked government:

1. Never let the right hand know about the dealings of the left. He hated staff conferences and committee meetings. He was the boss, he gave the orders. He met with people—heads of companies seeking multi-million-dollar contracts or department heads seeking patronage—on a one-to-one basis, usually in the subdued sanctuary of his inner office on the fifth floor of the old Hall. He never let a word leave the room. No one took notes, nothing was recorded or written down. Nixon could have learned a lesson about private dealings from Daley.

Critics who went to the sanctum sanctorum to confront him were usually in for a surprise. He flattered everyone. He listened, he nodded, he smiled and listened some more. People who wanted his blessing to run for office would present their case and see, in Daley's noncommittal directive to go out and see if they had support, a pleasant affirmation of their own desire to run. It was no such thing. Daley was a waiter a listener and a watcher. When he moved he moved swiftly, but it might take a long time for him to move.

He especially worked on legitimate power brokers in the other city that had stagnated in the Loop and on the lakefront. He made it clear to them he was pro-big business and he was pro-downtown. One of the solid achievements of his years was to halt the erosion of the city's center so common in other cities. The Loop revived under Daley; the stock exchanges grew; apartment living downtown took root; theater was encouraged and all the arts woke up. His support was sometimes subtle, sometimes not. When the chairman of Standard Oil of Indiana thought to move his headquarters out of the city, Daley convinced John Swearingen not only to stay in the Loop but to throw up a new eighty-story building to house the giant company. And it all worked one-on-one.

2. Working inside the Machine, Daley did not hesitate from the beginning to use his power. He held the jobs, all the jobs, not only as mayor but as chairman of the central committee. Not since Cermak had one man wielded such iron control of the Machine—and Cermak headed the Machine in a Depression. Daley rode the wave of prosperity in the country and rebuilt the city out of it.

Daley worked the details. A neighborhood pal and onetime driver, Matthew Danaher, kept an extensive card file for him listing jobs, favors, contracts and vote returns related to all the committeemen who courted him. (After Danaher's death, Daley picked a bright redheaded numbers man named Tom Donovan to do the same bookkeeping job.) He listened and he knew. Committeeman Joe Burke of the Canaryville Fourteenth Ward once left a meeting with Daley about jobs saying, "For God's sake, you wonder how he can run the city, keeping all that shit about how many jobs you've got in his head."

Like most successful men, he amazed his peers simply by working harder than they worked.

3. Daley made the Machine include. He included blacks, included the ethnics, included the old-timers and new-timers. Arvey never lost his job as national committeeman under Daley; there was no reason for Daley not to let him keep the title and influence. Daley created a palace guard of younger men (and the woman, Jane Byrne) who owed absolute loyalty to him, controlled no jobs, had no patronage or clout, who had never run for office—and yet were the very technocrats he needed to keep the city functioning smoothly. He made them and they knew it.

4. Daley was the perfect Machine boss in the sense that he imposed no ideas on others; he waited for their ideas. Chicago's turn as a boom town was over, had been over since the 1930s. But Daley saw other ways Chicago could succeed. The city had to attract new corporations and new jobs and give good service to do these things and that included holding down the tax rate. He held it down and it worked. The business climate of Chicago became easygoing. What the Man on Five said was the last word and you didn't have to pay off a clutch of aldermen to get a legitimate business deal made.

University of Chicago professor Edward C. Banfield detailed the way things worked under Daley in his admiring account, *Political Influence*. He said Daley's very indifference to ideas made it possible for him to get things done. He was the eternal catalyst. He would wait for the major interests involved in a project to fight their way to a compromise; then he would take credit for the compromise solution and push the project, satisfying all sides.[5]

The *Chicago Tribune*—through its permanent Springfield lobby in the form of its political editor, George Tagge—made it plain it wanted a giant exhibition hall in Chicago named for its late publisher, Colonel McCormick. Daley pushed his people in the legislature to get it done.

The University of Chicago wanted to create a viable neighborhood in the black ghetto that surrounded it through slum clearance and heavy code enforcement of housing. Daley got it done.

Unions made out; business made out; commerce made out. It was almost like the old days because the guy in city hall had the power to do things. And he let well enough alone—he did not reform the Machine, he let the "boys" keep their petty graft, influence and contract peddling.

He got on with the Outfit, seeing that the once minor Sicilian syndicate was now a national business, complex in its dealings. They controlled wards and votes and money. Daley let them alone, included them, but made them behave in Chicago. The First Ward, dominated by Outfit interests, flourished again under Committeeman John D'Arco—but they kept their lights under a bushel.

Daley ensured city control of what would become the world's busiest airport by conning the suburbs to sell the city a corridor of land to and around O'Hare Field. Thus, he added more jobs to the Machine pile. He induced the state to build a first-time, four-year branch of the University of Illinois on the West Side—and displaced a large number of Italian (and Outfit) voters in the process. Bill Thompson had called himself "The Builder," but he was a piker next to Daley.

Daley seemed a miracle worker next to the dithering men who ran cities like New York in the 1960s. But it was done with mirrors. A New York City did not share the burden of dealing with the poor; Chicago made the state share it. The state funded the city's charity hospital and the state handled welfare payments, not the city. The Chicago Park District,

Sanitary District, Public Building Commission, and the school board—all controlled by Daley and the Machine—were actually state creations on paper and had separate taxing districts. Daley was a master at getting somebody else to pick up the check, at shuffling responsibilities between one body and another. It was a bookkeeper's talent, and a highly useful one.

In fact, the singular achievement of the Daley years in an era of expanding federal subsidies was in glomming those subsidies for the city at no expense of power to the Machine. Daley always found a way to make someone else pay for it and give himself the credit as well.

In one five-year period in the sixties—because of Daley's enlightened investment policies—private interests poured five billion dollars into rebuilding the mile-square grid called the Loop.

He was not building for the ages but buying time. Critics of the Emerald City created by the Wizard of Bridgeport argued that a lot of Daley's work was illusion. It was. Politics is the art of illusion. If things seem good, they must be good. Nothing lasts forever. Was Chicago the city that works? It was if you thought so.

Why did Daley do it?

Tom Keane, his floor manager in the City Council who later went to jail for a time because he stole, once said, "Daley wanted power and I wanted money. We both got what we wanted."[6]

Daley was childishly simple. He loved the Chicago White Sox (a uniquely Chicago team in that they managed to throw a World Series). That was the South Side in him. But he always attended opening day for the Cubs on the North Side at Wrigley Field as well. When, after forty years, the Sox under Bill Veeck won a pennant in 1959, Daley told his pal, the supremely stupid Fire Commissioner Robert Quinn, to do something to celebrate. So Quinn, at the moment the pennant was clinched in the middle of a weekday August night, turned on all the city's air raid sirens. The end had come, amazed residents knew, and the Soviets were attacking. People poured out into the streets and flooded City Hall with pleas for Daley to stop the Russian invasion.

Daley gave such an illusion of supreme power after a time that people who should have known better really thought he was God. They expected solutions from him to problems that had no solution. For example, a half million rural and uneducated blacks flooded the city between 1950 and 1970, looking for jobs that had already fled to the suburbs and sun belts. Daley had no way to deal with them. The black tide created a backlash of middle-class whites fleeing the city and destroying the city tax base. Daley had no solutions to these problems, and he never really confronted the black-white problem in Chicago, preferring to ignore it.

Daley had the power for nearly twenty-two years, and the city underwent a change that is still not over. A new and elegant and integrated and powerful city has been growing inside the gaping wound of the larger city. The elegant city with its parkways, culture, restaurants and high-class jobs in high-class buildings reaches out north, south and west from the Loop for less than four miles in one direction, three in another, two in another. It is a smaller city but Daley helped create it. It is the city others can see when they look for Chicago, just as Manhattan becomes New York for visitors. It is brilliant, urban, sophisticated—much more so than the Loop that A. J. Liebling found thirty-five years ago. While satisfying the neighborhoods, the boy from the neighborhoods let a shining city be built on the pristine shoreline of Lake Michigan, and it is something to behold.

Perhaps the old city that still clings to this new city is like the dying skin of the caterpillar that must make way for the butterfly. The metaphor is not stretched and the butterfly grows more beautiful and costly every day.

Go down into an old city tavern these days, down the charming, tree-lined streets of the restored neighborhoods, go down where there is still beer and laughter and talk about the Cubs and Bears and Sox, where the ferns are hanging up to the skylights and the beautiful people inhabit the beautiful city. It is not a plastic city: It is very Chicago, very tough, very loud, very boastful. And the most boastful thing of all you will find is a common lithograph in taverns:

It shows a newspaper blowup of Daley with his chin jutting out and the large, childlike eyes staring off to the right, beyond the frame. The caption says: *Great City*. That is all. It is in all the old taverns, even today, more than a decade after the death of Daley.

15

Cracks, Reforms

CHICAGO HAD A RADICAL TRADITION WHOSE GROWTH PAR-
alleled that of the Machine. Chicago exported radicalism, and its influence reached around the world in time—but
the reformist zeal never seemed able to bore into the structure of the city where it was born. The conservative tradition
of the Midwest and the success of the Machine were too
much to overcome.

Chicago's radicalism took many forms, and its cast of char-
acters rarely could agree on much. There was the Chicago
union tradition: Anarchists and unionists staged the first
strike for the eight-hour work day at McCormick Reaper
Works in 1886. The Haymarket Riot of May 4 came out of

that strike, and the worldwide labor celebration of May Day memorializes what happened in Chicago on that day.

The International Workers of the World was formed in Chicago. The Wobblies reached their peak of organizing power in the years before World War I, but they still maintain headquarters in the city.

But despite its labor tradition, Chicago was never a full union town like New York. The unions have been concentrated in the building trades. Plenty of small factories have always operated with nonunion help and frequently with illegal immigrants, and sweatshops abounded.

Radicalism of a different sort was practiced by Saul Alinsky, a Chicago organizer who had the idea of neighborhoods in cities seizing power for the common good. His pioneer work was begun in 1939 in the impoverished immigrant neighborhood called Back of the Yards because it was behind the Union Stockyards on the South Side. The experiment worked—the neighborhood became a social and political power in the larger community of Chicago, demanding city services and getting them, policing itself and enforcing its own codes of cleanliness and building safety.

(The communelike approach became encrusted with age in time and the Back of the Yards Council, under co-founder Joe Meegan, became a slavish tool of the Machine as well as a device to keep blacks out of the community.)

Alinsky's school for radicals, located in classroom space above a tavern off Michigan and Grand, spread his ideas to the black community in the form of the pioneering Woodlawn Organization, which got federal monies in the 1960s to upgrade the hopeless slum of Woodlawn on the South Side. The American Indian community received Alinsky-style organizing help in the 1970s.

Radical ideas of education that were widely adopted else-

where were germinated in the University of Chicago by people like Robert Hutchins, though the university has since
turned to a more conservative curriculum. New ideas in law,
social service and writing started in Chicago—but then went
elsewhere for their full flowering.

But political radicalism finally took root in Chicago in the
1960s, largely because of Richard J. Daley. The Boss—as Mike
Royko dubbed him—became the living symbol of the entrenched establishment largely because of his control of the
Machine and his longevity in office. He acted as the lightning
rod of protest in a way that no other Machine leader had.

The Machine kept renewing itself under Daley with bright
young candidates and bright young technocrats coming into
the fold—but they came under the old rules of behavior.
Those who wanted new rules in politics were left outside, and
it was the outsiders who became dangerous to the Machine.
For example, the establishment Chicago Bar Association was
seriously challenged by the Chicago Council of Lawyers,
which had been set up by non-Machine attorneys unwilling
to go along with the old rules.

The ancient ward bosses like Paddy Bauler in the Forty-
third and Eddie Barrett in the Forty-fourth—the two most
radicalized of the new wards—were fading. Young lawyer
Bill Singer beat Barrett's Machine in 1969 and became a rare
thing, an independent alderman.

Chicago was changing, growing, becoming more sophisticated almost too quickly in the 1960s. The new urban voters
filling out precincts along the north lakefront could not be
bought with traditional Machine favors of better garbage
pickup and clean streets. They demanded clean streets the
way rich people can demand these things. Daley's Machine
tried to placate the wards of the North Side but it was never
enough.

The violence of the Democratic National Convention of 1968 crystallized the opposition to Daley and, by extension, to the vague thing called The Establishment. Daley had not invented the war in Vietnam (in fact, he opposed it privately) but he suffered the political fallout from it. The antiwar independent political movement coalesced behind a drive against the "fascists" in City Hall, the police, even the "fascist" newspapers.

Radicalized journalists on the city's four daily papers formed *The Chicago Journalism Review,* the first ever journalism review published by reporters in the country, and attacked the hands that fed them on a monthly basis. Fairness in the city room became a radical cause; for the first time, old-line reporters who covered Chicago politics were singled out for attack by their younger colleagues as much as the politicians were.

Daley got stubborn, held on and fought back. At one press conference, he shouted that there were crooks to be found everywhere, even at this press conference and, looking at the reporters, he said, "I could spit on some of them from here."

It was true. Jake Lingle, the *Tribune* reporter killed in a hit because of his mob connections in the Capone days, had his descendants in the press corps. Paddy Bauler still distributed gift watches and cash payouts to reporters who wrote stories about the good old bunch of rascals in City Hall. The boys in the Hall didn't see what these new kids working for the papers had to be so high and mighty about.

Chicago's reform currents were disparate but intent in the 1960s. The people Machine men called radicals were against more than they were for. They were against patronage, against the idea of a political Machine, against the war in Vietnam, against Richard Nixon, stuffing ballot boxes, segregated housing. The more numerous the reformers' causes, the larger the Machine's opposition became. Eventually Daley stopped trying to include the opposition. As he got older, he became encrusted with his own sense of certainty. Had the Machine ever been more powerful, done more good for the city? Look at the skyline of the Loop, look at the stunning influx of paper businesses downtown, the explosive growth of the commercial exchanges, the restoration of culture in the growth of experimental theater and music groups. As Daley phrased it after the convention violence, spitting out at the radicals, "What trees do they plant?"

There had always been areas of the city which refused to go along with Daley's vision of Chicago. The upper-middle-class "better element" that had traditionally dogged the Machine was still there, and growing larger and more sophisticated all the time.

Hyde Park, which had produced a long line of reformers from Charles Merriam through Paul Douglas and the lone opposition voice in Daley's City Council, Alderman Leon Despres, is an artificially integrated neighborhood controlled by the University of Chicago and surrounded on three sides by a large, poor black ghetto. Hyde Park continues to stay afloat in this black sea because of federal subsidies that helped the university buy up property and oversee urban renewal on a large scale in the 1950s and 1960s. It is this neighborhood, supported by its successful alliance with the Machine, that was to provide the manpower for the first long-lasting successful assaults on Daley and his pals.

A young attorney, a product of the University of Chicago, had the misfortune to run for a seat in the 1969 Illinois Constitutional Convention. Michael Shakman ran against three other people in his Hyde Park District. He lost to the Machine candidate, a black woman lawyer named Odas Nicholson.

Shakman felt certain that he would have been the better man to help revise the state's outdated constitution. The loss rankled, and he attributed it to Nicholson's support by the Machine's money and precinct captains. The precinct captains who had turned out the vote for Nicholson were city workers paid with city tax money to electioneer. Was that fair? Was that just? Shakman thought it wasn't, and he and a few friends talked the matter over and decided to do something that turned out to be the most radical act of all.

One morning in 1969, Shakman filed a suit in U.S. District Court on Dearborn Street in the Loop. In precise legal language, the suit stated all that was wrong with machine politics in the view of Shakman and his reformer friends. Shakman cut open the machine in his suit and laid bare its heart. Patronage, he argued, with stunning naïveté, was illegal. It kept people like him from getting into office because it paid precinct workers tax dollars to do political work for people like Odas Nicholson.

Lots of liberal lawsuits were filed all the time. Independent political strategist Don Rose once called them "guerilla lawfare." But the Shakman suit challenged the very nature and logic of the political machine. The Machine exists on jobs. It controls jobs; it controls the people who hold the jobs. Control enough jobs and enough people and you can have enough workers to elect the people you pick for office—or, at least, you can control the primary process. Lose control of workers and jobs and you lose the control first implemented by Roger Sullivan and George Brennan with their 1916 invention of the "committeeman's letter" and a Democratic central committee controlling apportionment of the pie.

While the suit was finding its way through the court system, the radical reformers mounted a variety of assaults upon Daley's City Hall and the friends of the Machine. The warfare made Chicago politics interesting. It became the subject of street theater, and the cafes, saloons and restaurants were full of heated political arguments night after night.

Blacks were slow to be radicalized. Just as they had been the last Republicans left in Chicago, they were the last to challenge the Machine. Harold Washington, one of the young black lawyers who had risen to power in the Dawson organization, was still a holdout defender of Machine politics and patronage: "Patronage helped other ethnic groups. Why should it be denied use by my people?" he asked.

But the black flashpoint was reached with the 1968 riot after Martin Luther King's death, the police response and, finally, the December 1969 raid on the Black Panther party headquarters on the West Side.

Police from State's Attorney Edward Hanrahan's office raided the building after the FBI gave them information that the Panthers were hoarding weapons there. The cops broke into the apartment while its occupants were asleep, opened fire and ended up killing two young Panthers whose bodies were found on bloody mattresses.

The police insisted they had fired in self-defense, but when it was established that they had come in shooting, Ed Hanrahan, who loyally defended his men, was left to twist slowly in the wind.

Blacks of all political opinions saw the attack as another example of Daley Machine racism striking at people because of skin color. But Daley thought black opinion was well under control. Bill Dawson had died in 1970, and the black wards were rudderless while Washington and Ralph Metcalfe and others grabbed for power. But Dawson had left behind plenty of heirs to fill the seats of power allotted to blacks by the Machine, and Daley had confidence that the "race men" like Harold Washington, with their overheated rhetoric about

"plantation politics," would scarcely make a dent in the old
Machine alliance that had proved successful for so long.

Thus Daley was genuinely surprised at the uproar that followed Hanrahan's routine slating for reelection in 1972.
Hanrahan had become a symbol and a focus for all the discon-
tent that had been building up in black Chicago. Daley was a
stubborn man, but he knew a lot about damage control. He
called the slating committee back together—an unprecedented act—dumped Hanrahan and picked noncontroversial
Judge Raymond Berg to defuse the race for Cook County
state's attorney.

All hell broke loose: Hanrahan refused to be dumped. He
announced that he would run against Berg and the Machine.
And the independents of the North Side really made it a
donnybrook by naming Donald Page Moore—a wild-eyed
radical lawyer by all Machine standards—to run against both
of them.

It was a strange, surrealistic primary race in the spring of
1972. Moore, Berg and Hanrahan frequently found themselves debating each other on the same platform. Hanrahan
even crashed the St. Patrick's Day parade that spring, step-
ping jauntily down State Street in a hat and stick. As he
walked past the reviewing stand where the stunned Daley sat,
he doffed his hat—and a dove flew out. Daley got an embarrassing fit of the giggles while Hanrahan accomplished the
equivalent of cocking his snoot at the Machine.

Donald Moore was an all-out debater. He said: "I'm just an
old anti-Machine kamikaze pilot. Stuff my sinuses with ex-
plosives and aim me at City Hall."

Moore had money, something independents usually
lacked, and the anti-Machine crowd was in full throat. On the
North Side, the Bill Singer faction was taking the Machine as
a model for political organization, using ideologically com-

mitted volunteers instead of paid precinct captains. This was the beginning of the Independent Precinct Organization, which for a few years was more powerful than the Machine in the Forty-third and Forty-fourth wards. Organized block by block, IPO had its precinct workers on the street, passing out literature and turning out the vote on Election Day, in an attempt to fight the real Machine with a reform Machine built on precisely the people the old-style pols had decreed could never count in politics.

This was the year that Daley and his delegation would be kicked out of the Democratic Convention controlled by George McGovern and replaced with the likes of Bill Singer and Jesse Jackson. Nineteen seventy-two was a bad year for the Machine. Dan Walker, a corporation lawyer who had scratched at the doors of Machine power for years, had turned a new leaf in 1968 when asked to write a federal report on who caused the street riots at the convention. He decided the police had caused the riots and Daley exploded, but Walker became the darling of the radicals. He won the Democratic primary for governor and walked his way to office in the fall (by literally walking up and down the state, soliciting votes, and looking like a man of the people in his red bandana and blue jeans). Populism was in the throes of discovering Levis.

Hanrahan beat Moore and the Machine candidate, Berg, in the primary—but he was a vulnerable candidate the Machine had not wanted. Hanrahan, son of the Machine, had defeated the Machine in its own primary, just as Walker did (coming from a different part of the political spectrum). The Machine shuddered at what was happening to it. The worst came in the general election. McGovern lost. Walker won. And Bernard Carey, a Republican who got support from Moore as well as covert support in the black wards from Ralph Metcalfe, beat Hanrahan. The days of "plantation politics" in the black wards when black votes were docilely turned over to Machine candidates of whatever color appeared ended.

For the first time in the Daley years, the Machine was losing badly on too many fronts. It became defensive and the closed doors were shut tight. The Chicago press—including the now-powerful local television news—was routinely anti-Machine in its reporting, correcting years of pro-Machine drift in a few months of heavy anti-Machine, anti-Daley, coverage. Television, in particular, battled the power of the precinct workers. Jane Byrne would say later, "Television is the new precinct captain."

The city base of power had shifted dramatically, and it had nothing to do with the efficiency of the Machine. There were factors it could not control. The influx of blacks created a wide expansion of the black community south and west across middle-class white neighborhoods. Whites fled to the suburbs and turned their backs on city politics. What could a Machine do when it was based on the city and its supporters had now fled beyond the city limits?

But the real change in the way the Machine ran things occurred under Daley's nose in federal court, as a result of the Shakman case. The reason the suit had such impact is to be found in political scientist Milton Rakove's description of how things worked: "It is impossible to make an accurate analysis of the number of patronage positions distributed by the Cook County Democratic central committee to loyal workers, precinct captains and supporters, but a fairly educated guess would be that there may be approximately 30,000 patronage positions available. . . . They are located in agencies ranging from approximately 70 jobs in the county coroner's office to approximately 6,000 jobs in the city of Chicago's departments and commissions. There are also many thousands of jobs in private industry throughout the Chicago metropolitan area which require the sponsorship of Democratic ward committeemen. . . .

"If each job is worth 10 votes in an election, the Machine has a running start of approximately 300,000 votes derived directly from the patronage system."[1]

But between 1969, when Shakman filed the suit, and 1979, a series of "Shakman decrees" were issued in federal district court that slowly and surgically cut the heart of the Machine.

The first agreements signed by county officers ensured that they would not fire people for failure to do political work. The Cook County Sheriff, Richard Elrod, refused to sign, but the courts later held it was illegal for him to fire such people anyway.

Slowly and surely, the spread of Shakman protection—a sort of court-ordered job tenure—moved from office to office. By 1979, U.S. Judge Nicholas Bua was interpreting the growing Shakman consensus on job protection to mean that you could not even hire people based on the idea of political clout—which struck at the heart of the "committeeman's letter" system of hiring.

The Shakman decrees did not destroy the Machine, but they weakened it. The people who hope to keep the Machine alive—and that includes all of Daley's successors as mayor—keep fighting. Harold Washington, for example, went to court to argue that he needed an additional 1,350 patronage jobs to help him run the government, despite the protected pre-Washington people who were still in City Hall.

Starting from the single flashpoint of the 1968 Democratic Convention and fueled by Machine stubbornness that came from Daley down, the people the Machine called radicals finally had their day in Chicago politics. In the end, the Machine tore itself apart, but that was possible only because of

the continued pressure from outside—from disappointed office seekers like Michael Shakman, from self-described ka-
mikazes like Donald Page Moore, from turncoats like Dan
Walker.

Daley, bewildered as a bull elephant caught in snares, bellowed and struggled against the change, but there was really
nothing to be done. The world had changed; the sea change
had finally rolled across the shore and drowned King Lear.

16

After the End

THE CITY WAS PRETTY ON DALEY'S LAST DAY, LIKE A YOUNG woman cast into premature mourning.

Outside City Hall, in the giant Civic Center plaza, Picasso's statue of a dog kept watch. The city workers, by tradition, had erected the city Christmas tree, a splendid thing composed of dozens of giant balsams stuck into telephone poles that stand five stories high. The tree was covered with lights and the promise of the season.

It was December 20, 1976.

Tiny Italian lights in the thousands also sparkled in bare branches along North Michigan Avenue, all the way up to Water Tower Place. Salvation Army Santas rang bells in the

Loop and police whistles blown to direct traffic added to the gay sound. Such a pretty, mournful sort of morning, with the threat of rain in the air and the gray lake pounding at the breakers on the lakefront.

Daley had been driven out to the neglected Tenth Ward on the far Southeast Side of the city—almost at the Indiana line—to dedicate a new Park District gymnasium. It was such a little thing to do, but it showed the way the Machine worked in those last days, the way it had always worked in a line stretching back to Cermak and, before him, Roger Sullivan and George Brennan, the godfathers of organized politics.

When Daley went to the gym he was demonstrating the clout of Ed Kelly, head of the Park District, to get the Big Man to visit the ward. He was also mending fences with Edward Vrdolyak, the maverick Croatian alderman of the ward who had tested the Machine a few times but still stayed inside the fold.

Vrdolyak oozed the sincerity of a dentist, and his power base in South Chicago (as the district was called) was too poor to spring him to bigger things. He worked hard in the Machine and figured, as Daley had before him, that hard work would bring him power simply because most people do not work hard. Daley admired that in him; it was something of himself; and so he came.

On the last day of his life, Daley could contemplate a changed city with satisfaction; with less satisfaction, he could reflect on a changed city's new politics. Two years before, for the first time in his life, he had been hospitalized. Doctors had operated on a narrowing artery in his neck that fed his brain. Though the surgery had been successful, the intimation of mortality had moved Daley to sentimentality. His press conferences now were sometimes rambling affairs, full of sentiment and tears and thoughts of God and death expressed in traditional Irish terms. He spoke of affection and friendships as though he were losing these things.

He was not. The city loved him, even that part of the city that did not love him in politics. He was the real and shining presence of the city in itself and in the world.

Daley had turned over his card index file and more of the details of running Machine and city to unelected Tom Donovan, the bright boy from Bridgeport with red hair and more phone lines than anyone else in city government. Daley was like a king in his dotage, traveling through his kingdom, seeing his subjects, nodding at them, acting as the symbol of the power that he really did not possess anymore.

While Daley sat in the gym watching the ceremony, he felt the pains in his chest. He had one of his bodyguards (plainclothes policemen) call Dr. Thomas Coogan, his physician. He wanted to see him.

Coogan waited for him in his office on Michigan Avenue. He quickly read the physical signs and told the seventy-six-year-old mayor he would have to go into the hospital at once.

It was not to be. Coogan left Daley for a moment to call a member of the Daley family and tell the news.

In that moment, Daley suffered a massive heart attack, fell to the floor and died almost immediately, though paramedics from the fire department worked on him for a long time after that.

THE WORD SPREAD QUICKLY BUT QUIETLY, AS THOUGH NEWS OF the death of the king might imperil the kingdom.

Colonel Jack Reilly, Daley's one-eyed coat holder and the man in charge of dyeing the Chicago River green every St. Patrick's Day (it is still done), was met by a clot of reporters in City Hall who wanted to know if the rumor was true that

Daley was dead. Reilly denied it vehemently, as though it was a radical plot to discredit the Machine. But the reporters saw the truth in the tears of the secretaries filing in and out of the Mayor's Office, the shuttered suite on the fifth floor of the Hall. They saw it when Mike Bilandic, alderman from Daley's home ward, broke off a meeting of the City Council Finance Committee to go to the Mayor's office on a signal from Tom Donovan.

Donovan was the key player in those hours after Daley's death. He was already thinking about what would happen next. Daley had left no indication of a successor; the grab for power might prove fatal to the Machine. The players had to be assembled and new rules had to be drawn up to keep the Machine intact. The radical barbarians were at the gates.

Donovan was a technocrat, with no political power base now that Daley was dead; but he was clever enough to realize it. He summoned Ed Vrdolyak. Vrdolyak was as smart as he was, and he too had a reason to think long and hard about the new arrangements that would be made after Daley. Vrdolyak had an obscure power base which might ensure him no status at all in post-Daley Chicago. Working together, Vrdolyak and Donovan came up with a plan that might salvage their power and even increase it: They would put into the mayor's chair a seat-warmer, someone whose strings they could pull from behind a curtain.

The man they picked was Mike Bilandic, another Daley creation, a Bridgeporter whose loyalty to Daley had gotten him an aldermanic seat and the chairmanship of the City Council Finance Committee. Bilandic had the face of a basset hound with large watery blue eyes. The blue eyes were filled with tears that day in the mayor's office. The tears dried, however, when he heard the terms of the deal that Vrdolyak and Donovan proposed. He would be anointed Daley's successor as mayor; the others would handle the little details like patronage and political organization.

Bilandic's loyalties stopped at death's door. The new terms would freeze out the Daley family, and Bilandic knew it. Bill Daley, the smartest of the old man's sons, said later that Mike Bilandic was the last guy his father would have thought of as a successor.

It could be said that Bilandic would have been last on just about anybody's list of possibilities. He was an amiable enough man, immersed in details, with the flat, unemphatic speech of a man who finds public attention puzzling. He and the flamboyant, wisecracking Vrdolyak were Croatians; it made a tie of sorts, but two less similar personalities could hardly be imagined.

The anti-Daley family crowd gathered as quickly to put together a new Machine as the Daley family gathered to bury the old Boss. Eddie Burke signed on as a fixer and co-conspirator with Vrdolyak and Donovan.

Burke, like Vrdolyak, was raw and tough. When his father, Joe Burke, died and the post of committeeman and alderman fell vacant in Canaryville, nobody gave Eddie anything. Eddie was a cop then, street-smart and cold-eyed and only twenty-four years old. He never forgot his enemies who had gathered at his father's wake in "little clusters" around the funeral parlor, "discussing who would get what. It was almost like the Roman soldiers casting lots for the garments under the cross at the crucifixion."

Not quite. Joe Burke wasn't Christ and Eddie Burke wasn't St. Paul. He tore the organization apart, put himself in charge and punished his enemies. Now he was doing the same thing he accused others of doing, only with a new set of Roman soldiers who had Irish and Croatian surnames.

THEY BURIED DALEY OUT OF THE CHURCH OF THE NATIVITY IN Bridgeport where he had gone to daily Mass. President Ford mourned the mayor, and so did all the men of power in the country. Some of the tears were even genuine. Daley had been loved, by some people—and that is a rare enough thing in a politician to be remarked upon.

But while the city mourned, the City Council went on with the business of keeping the Machine rolling. The grab for power was on. Donovan and Vrdolyak, Burke and Bilandic had cut their deals but there were other wards to be heard from.

Wilson Frost, a fleshy-faced black alderman from the Third Ward and another protégé of the Dawson machine, had been a Machine regular and president pro tem under Daley. He got the job as pro tem because, as private corporations know, when the boardroom is white it looks better to have a black at the reception desk out front. The job was utterly meaningless. Forty-eight hours after Daley dropped dead, Frost dropped a bombshell.

He called in the press and announced that he was interim mayor. He said he had read the rules of the Council and all the regulations and that, as second officer to the mayor, he succeeded the mayor.

Vrdolyak and Donovan were momentarily confused. He couldn't do this, could he? A black mayor? (Students of Chicago politics are always amazed at the complete lack of understanding among Machine powers of rules of procedure. It owes to perpetual neglect of such rules in the actual running of the city. In effect, Chicago has no rules.)

But it turned out that Wilson Frost was only kidding. Rather than leading a black revolution, he could be bought off—he was like Roger Sullivan in the old days when he pulled a mace by inventing the Ogden Gas Company to be bought out by Peoples Gas.

The deal was cut: Frost was given the chairmanship of the powerful Finance Committee. The post had been the springboard of wealth and power for years—it had made Jake Arvey powerful under Kelly and Tom Keane rich under Daley.

Bilandic was named mayor by the council within a week of Daley's death. The outsiders did not understand it—Bilandic was seen as warming the seat of power for Daley's son, Richard M., to take over. It wasn't that way at all; Richie was frozen out, the whole Daley family was out. Enemies were made and new friends joined hands in those few frantic days of grabbing power. Daley's Machine was a thing of the past; it remained to be seen if a new Machine could hold it together.[1]

17
Fighting Jane

JANE BYRNE WAS LACE-CURTAIN IRISH WITH A NEED TO NURSE grudges and a convenient memory. She was also a clown in the tradition of Big Bill Thompson and used her clownishness to crack what turned out to be an eggshell-thin Machine.

Born Jane Burke, she grew up in a big house in Sauganash, a snooty neighborhood on the Northwest Side. Her parish was Queen of Heaven, where the rich Irish go on Sunday to pray for forgiveness for the money they have made all week, and also for the way they have made it.

Jane Burke was good at her schoolwork but she had the ambition common to most girls of her time—to marry well.

After graduating from Barat College, which then had a reputation for being a party school, she married William Byrne, a Notre Dame graduate and son of a wealthy Cleveland family. Byrne was planning to become a lawyer, but he was killed in a freakish plane crash while he was a marine pilot. He left Jane Byrne a widow with a young daughter, Kathy.

Jane met Richard Daley through her family and church connections at a number of the functions at which wealthy Irish would meet and press the flesh of the Machine lords and fill out checks for favors yet to be received. Jane said later that Daley told her to "look him up" for a job, not realizing he said that to lots of people.

Left alone with an infant daughter, she taught herself lessons of bitterness, cursed fate that made her a widow and alienated herself from friends. She briefly worked for the John F. Kennedy campaign in Chicago—her sister brought her in as a volunteer—and later made much more of it than there was. Jane Byrne was always very good at fabricating large lies from little truths. This is the way it worked with Kennedy.

The presidential candidate came into Chicago to kiss Daley's ring and to thank the little people who were working to get him elected. Crowded into the Kennedy campaign office were all the workers. Kennedy said a few words and posed for pictures. Jane Byrne edged her way to the front with baby Kathy in her arms and either she or one of the photographers suggested JFK hold the child on his lap. Kennedy did the Kennedy grin, held the perplexed Kathy a moment and a myth was born in a photograph that intimated that Jane Byrne was close to the Kennedy family. It wasn't so, but then so much of Jane's story of herself wasn't so.

Byrne got a variety of small jobs inside the Machine because of Daley's clout. She was just another technocrat with no clout of her own—she never rang doorbells, despite her claim later that she did, and she was never elected to anything—and she worked about as hard at her job as the average payroller.

In 1968, Daley put Byrne in charge of the scandal-ridden but unimportant Department of Weights and Measures. He wanted to clean up the image of the smallest of the city's fifty-eight departments. The papers were alleging (and it was true) that inspectors were approving short-weighting of customers in stores and meat markets, particularly in black neighborhoods.

The only thing on the square in Weights and Measures when Jane walked into the job was the doorway. She did a credible job of cleaning up the department and she got herself noticed in the press. Daley liked that and he liked her. He sometimes called her in for a private chat in his office as he did with other department heads. She made more of this than there was, of course, as a good politician will do.

Byrne, who dressed like a teenager in short skirts, ruffled blouses and heavy makeup beneath her dyed-blond hair, started dating the most notorious bachelor in the press room at City Hall. Jay McMullen worked for the failing *Chicago Daily News*. He was a great pal of Paddy Bauler and people like developer Harry Chaddick and he frankly admired the Machine crowd to the extent of cheerleading the Machine in print.

Jane and Jay hit it off and Jay saw to it that Jane got good ink in the *Daily News*. In a curious way, the afternoon *News* wagged the tails of the more powerful morning newspapers which had to follow up on its stories with afternoon headlines, no matter how outrageous.

When Daley died in late 1976, Jay McMullen saw to it that Jane Byrne's memoirs of her intimate relationship with Daley

reached print. Jane remembered a lot. She remembered
Daley musing about his illness and his coming last days and
how he wanted Jane to run for higher office, perhaps to
become mayor someday. She remembered Daley's special
protection for her in the Machine when others were jealous
of her honesty and power.

Remember, remember, remember: She was driving guys
like Bilandic nuts. Until they realized that—hey!—the broad
didn't have any clout anymore. Daley was dead, wasn't he?

But Jay McMullen canonized his girlfriend in the columns
of the *Daily News* every chance he got and it continued to
irritate the string pullers behind Bilandic. Jay did it for fun;
he was a fun guy and a rogue in the Paddy Bauler school of
geniality.

He used to brag to his pals in the Hall that Jane gave him
a lot of scoops. Three months after Daley's death, he was
boasting in *Esquire* magazine (in a story by Eleanor Randolph)
about his role as City Hall Don Juan:

"I've screwed girls who work at City Hall for years. There
was a day when I could roll over in bed in the morning and
scoop the *Tribune*. Anybody who wouldn't screw a dame for
a story is disloyal to his paper."[1]

Despite these lapses in taste, Jay continued to get along
great with Jane. They were made for each other.

BILANDIC WON ELECTION AS MAYOR ON HIS OWN IN 1977, BUT
he was weak. The black community didn't like him much—
there is a strong antipathy between blacks and Eastern European ethnics in Chicago. Next, a few Machine pols like
Roman Pucinski were even considering running against the
Donovan-Vrdolyak-Burke combine. Needless to say, screw-
ing the Daley family had not endeared Bilandic to any of the

old Daley supporters either. Bilandic's weakness should have made the Machine more uneasy than it did. But then, the Machine was in a pretty weak condition itself, so weak that an inconsequential taxicab caper led to its demise.

THE CAB MEDALLIONS IN CHICAGO ARE MOSTLY CONTROLLED BY two firms that are part of the Checker Corporation—Checker cabs and Yellow cabs. The company always had friends inside the Hall. In the old days, before he went to jail, Tom Keane—Daley's floor leader—took care of cab company concerns, like new rate increases and putting the squeeze on the few independents. When Keane went to jail, Vrdolyak took over as the cab company's man inside the Machine.

Jane Byrne, as Consumer Sales Commissioner (the new name for the Department of Weights and Measures) was in charge of regulating cab companies. She started pushing stringent enforcement of rules. It annoyed the cab companies. It annoyed Vrdolyak.

Byrne put together a new and comprehensive cab ordinance that she claimed would regulate the cab companies for the public benefit. According to Byrne, the day after Bilandic was sworn in as mayor of Chicago on his own—August 1977— she and Tom Donovan went to Bilandic's office in the Hall to talk about a proposed taxi fare increase. Ed Bedore, city budget director, was also present.

The meeting was interrupted when a group of protestors showed up in the hall outside the fifth floor suite of offices to show their displeasure about the latest city school desegregation plan. Bilandic said they should find a more quiet place to talk about such an important matter as a taxi fare increase and he suggested that the four slip out the back way.

Surrealism intrudes again on this account: The four got into Bilandic's city limousine and took a drive out to the Southwest Side, to Midway Airport. Why? Why not? It was private and away from prying ears.

During the drive, Jane Byrne said that Tom Donovan got itchy fingers, picked up the car phone and called his office to tell his secretary to find Edward Vrdolyak and get "his people" out to Midway Airport for a meeting on cabs.

They got to the airport, found an empty office to wait in and waited. After a while, Jerry Feldman, president of Checker cab, showed up along with Corporation Counsel Bill Quinlan. They said they were waiting for Don Reuben, the firm's lawyer (who never did show up). After a long while in which nothing happened—it might have been a Bergman film—they all got up, went back to their cars and left.

What did this mean?

Jane Byrne said it meant that the taxi fare increase had been "greased" by Bilandic and Vrdolyak on behalf of the cab companies. Because the cab ordinance was set up in such a way that any fare increase had to be justified by declining profit margins, presetting the fare increase (with the evidence to follow later) would be illegal.

Byrne worked with the press to manipulate the players in the taxi fare drama. At one time, she was leaking versions of her account to three reporters. The most gullible of the papers was the *Chicago Daily News*. The paper was dying, being killed by the inept management of Marshall Field's hirelings (they also owned the profitable *Sun-Times*), and the paper assumed a deathbed coloration in those last weeks.

Jane Byrne gave the *News* her account of a taxi fare "fix" by Bilandic and his pals Vrdolyak and Burke, as well as Don Reuben, the *Tribune* lawyer, and also the Checker lawyer.

The accounts were drawn from a secret diary she had kept. It recorded such things as her presence in a room full of fixers discussing the taxi fix. A lot of Machine people were stupid, but hardly people like Vrdolyak. Yet despite the poverty of Byrne's version, the papers loved it because they loved the scandal it implied.

Bilandic fired Jane Byrne. Byrne took a lie detector test to prove she was telling the truth. She passed. Bilandic took a lie detector test to prove *he* was telling the truth. He passed. Less than a year after Daley's death, the great Machine resembled nothing so much as a second-rate comedy troupe playing in a tank town.

The *Daily News* died on March 4, 1978, loudly mourned as a great paper (though it had long abandoned its lofty past for a sleazy present). McMullen lost his job, and both he and Jane were unemployed. They did a brave thing: They got married and Byrne announced she was going to run against the Machine for mayor.

They had no money and fewer friends. Jane mortgaged her family house. Jay borrowed against his sinking fund which was in the process of sinking.

Jay taught Jane about the press. The press in Chicago was no more of a bully than the press in other cities but Jay had worked as one of the bully boys and knew how to turn the papers to his own purpose. He thought up imaginative press releases for Jane, quoting her as calling Bilandic, Burke and Vrdolyak "a cabal of evil men" bent on raping the city.

The cynical corps of reporters who covered politics were amused by Byrne and made fun of her through the long year of campaigning she undertook in 1978, prior to the February 1979 mayoral primary. They didn't think she had a chance against the Machine or Bilandic—but she was funny in her denunciation of Machine evils. She was good copy and good for a forty-five-second clip on the 6 P.M. news shows. Mc-Mullen saw to that.

Byrne was that rare woman who is very good at emotional confrontation. She did not hesitate ever when attacking reporters at her press conferences or confronting one of the Machine bullies on his own turf.

She also represented a new challenge to the Machine that echoed back to the days of Bill Thompson when things had also been up for grabs. Back then, the Democrats had the careful self-controlled organization designed by Sullivan and Brennan. Thompson had a pair of rats in cages and complete and charismatic unscrupulousness. The Sullivan-Brennan Machine had been too narrow to beat the demogogic appeal of a Thompson. And the Vrdolyak-Bilandic-Burke Machine was too narrow as well. Demagoguery won the day for Byrne—along with television and winter.

WINTERS IN CHICAGO ARE NOT NEARLY AS BIG OR BAD AS Chicagoans boast they are. The average winter snowfall is forty-four inches, less than half that of Buffalo, New York. The city is rarely paralyzed by storms or cold.

But God was not on the side of the Machine in the winter of 1978–79. Before it was over, nearly ninety inches of snow would fall on the city. Before it was over, O'Hare Airport would paralyze the nation's air traffic by being closed for nearly six days. Trains would stop running, El lines would virtually cease to exist, streets would be made impassable for weeks. Highways were closed and littered for days with abandoned cars. The cold and snow shut down the city like a death sentence.

To have lived in the city that winter was to endure two months of a frozen hell. Workers spent hours getting to the

Loop, only to find their offices closed. Commerce slowed to a trickle; stores went out of business because they could not generate cash sales.

On the West Side, a crazed commuter seized control of an El train parked at the Lake Street terminus in Oak Park and took it for a ride across the city. He made all the stops and took on grateful passengers. The police finally caught him at the far South Side terminus of the line and transit officials said he had done a good job in moving traffic.

On the South Side, a man running a snowplow to clear streets went temporarily insane and smashed a line of parked cars blocking his efforts to clear streets.

The city's Department of Streets and Sanitation was stunned by the fury of the unexpected winter. One worker said, "It was like moving cement."

While winter wrought havoc, Jay McMullen's purple prose continued to color Jane Byrne's press statements: "These sinister apostles of self-aggrandizement not only present a clear and present danger to good government, but they threaten to perpetuate themselves in the seats of the mighty and I believe present a menace that calls for a united response from the citizens of Chicago."

Bilandic messed up the snow emergency. He dithered at the helm and no one helped him very much. He was told by his staff that drivers could park their cars in school parking lots in the city to get them off the streets. He announced this to the press—and then had to retreat when it turned out no one had plowed the school lots. And then the CTA announced it would run its elevated trains past stops in black neighborhoods in order to get people into downtown from outlying white stops in a hurry. Blacks began to turn their wrath on the mild little man in City Hall. He was in it up over his head and the stuff he was in was snow.

Jane's "staff" was a collection of outsiders and anti-Machine stalwarts like independent strategist Don Rose, who advised her to stop dying her hair and try to look like a normal person by wearing a wig. She did. She had scraped up $87,000 by winter and she put it all in TV ads.

Mike Royko, an early Jane Byrne supporter, advised her discreetly through his public columns to hit at the issue of the way the city mishandled the winter disaster. Rose caught the message, made the commercials center on brave Jane Byrne standing in the street, saying none of this would have happened if Mayor Daley were still alive. People wanted to believe that. They would believe anything to stop this horrible winter.

Then the papers revealed a $90,000 "snow emergency plan" awarded by contract to former Deputy Mayor Ken Sain. (The brilliant plan said things like snow should be plowed off streets after storms and El lines should keep running.)

Bilandic never knew what hit him. He was on the ropes but he staggered back into the fray. He had his TV commercials too, but they were not about winter. They featured his patrician wife, Heather, moving about her home like Jackie Kennedy, talking in polished tones rarely heard beyond Astor Street. She was blonde and beautiful and you knew it never snowed on her parade. The neighborhoods—white, black and Hispanic—were beside themselves with fury at this stupid Machine that couldn't even clean up the snow.

Bilandic fell on his own lance days before the election in a pep rally for Machine precinct captains. In a long and rambling speech of the sort once favored by Daley, he spoke of his frustrations and made strange comparisons about his persecution by the press and other critics:

"We've withstood challenges in the past. They've tried to

take it away from us before, but they couldn't. In the early history of Christianity, you see a leader starting with twelve disciples. They crucify the leader and make martyrs of the others. And what was the result? Christianity is bigger and stronger than it was before!"

Bilandic as Christ; the Machine as the Church. It was embarrassing and some of the captains in the audience averted their eyes. Bilandic began to cry as he continued: "It's our turn to be in the trenches, to see if we are made of the same stuff as the early Christians, the persecuted Jews, the proud Poles, the blacks and Latinos."

He went on to cite chaos in Iran and Cambodia and how it related to Chicago, though it was not snowing in either of the other two locales. "The same seeds of subversion are being planted right here in Chicago," he said. "The same attempt to destroy is just as strong here today as it is in these foreign intrigue situations."

It should be noted that Bilandic's incoherent tirade only reflected the tirades that used to come from Daley, who once said, "They have vilified me and crucified me and, yes, even criticized me."[2] But then, Daley made the trains run on time.

George Dunne had taken over as chairman of the party after Daley's death. He was a mild, skeptical man in the mold of George Brennan of an earlier machine. He thought Bilandic had made a fool of himself throughout his campaign and he thought that Vrdolyak and Burke were not competent to help him win. Still, he told Bilandic he would get 350,000 votes in the primary and that was usually enough to win.

In fact, on primary day at the end of February, 1979—the day that cracked the Machine all to hell, once and for all—Bilandic got 396,134 votes.

But the angry city had stopped believing in the invincible

Machine and 412,909 turned out for Jane Byrne and that was it. Jane Byrne was boss and on that night, in the ballroom of the Ambassador East Hotel, surrounded by a strange collection of firemen who wanted contracts, radicals who wanted reform and outsiders who wanted in, she said it plain, "Yes, I beat the Machine."

It was absolutely true. She had beaten it and, in fact, destroyed it, though she did not know it then, as Vrdolyak did not, nor even George Dunne. Like a decapitated chicken, the Machine twitched on for a few years with nervous life. But it was really dead. It was dead because of the Shakman decrees, because a puny opponent like Jane Byrne (albeit a great campaigner) could beat the captains and the ward committeemen, because the quality of leadership was too parochial to see a larger common good. The Machine was dead because the city didn't need it anymore and finally realized it. Because the captive working class had fled the old ethnic wards and the captive blacks had broken their chains in self-interest. It was dead because it was too narrow to mean very much anymore to anyone.

18
Lords and Lady

IT WAS ONE OF THE MANY IRONIES OF JANE BYRNE'S VICTORY that the destroyer of the Machine was one of the few people who truly believed in its glory. In a time that seemed to call for the quiet certainty of a George Washington, Jane Byrne could see nothing but the dream of being a new George III. Only it was not George III Jane Byrne wanted to be, but Richard J. Daley. She did not understand that the time of Machine rule was over, that the fragmentation of the races and the pileup of economic woes had doomed that kind of government. Byrne did not want a new coalition, even though a new coalition was what had put her in office. She wanted

the Machine back in its full state, as it had been in the time of
its greatest glory.

And so in the first few months following her victory, her
plans began to change. She held long, serious meetings with
reform leaders like the scholarly Martin Oberman from the
Forty-third Ward; these men then rushed elatedly out of her
office to busy themselves setting up plans for her takeover of
the City Council in the name of reform interests. And then,
when they called back to report on their progress, she would
not speak to them.

She hired academics to study ways to reform city government; months later they resigned in noisy protest. The way
was clear by then: Jane Byrne had embraced the "cabal of
evil men"—the men she believed still constituted a Machine—
and they had embraced her.

But the day was past for such antics. The new alliance of
Jane Byrne, ex-reformer, and the Machine forces could not
be anything but farce now. And Jane was perfectly suited to
playing the main part in a farce.

Byrne was, as Bill Thompson had been, bored by the in-
tricacies of administration. Like Thompson, she liked parties, fairs, carnivals, events which showed to advantage her
intention to lead Chicago to "world class city" status. She
liked to dress up. A famous photo shows her and her daughter Kathy dressed in brief suntops wearing sunglasses and
fedoras in imitation of the Blues Brothers, as the movie stars
John Belushi and Dan Aykroyd look on.

Promises had tripped easily off Jane Byrne's lips, but the
fulfilling of them was something else. She had promised to
reform the taxi ordinance; she did not. She had promised to
reform the police; instead, she threw it into confusion, going
through three police chiefs in four years. She promised the

fire department a union contract in exchange for election support by the rank and file, who indeed had been some of her most dedicated precinct workers; instead, she denied ever having said such a thing, and the fire department went on strike for the first time in the city's history.

She had run on a program of giving fair services to the black community; she turned her back on the black wards and packed the school board with white members at a time when the schools were mostly black. Leaving Vrdolyak in firm control of the City Council and its committee structure, she eventually settled on another of the "cabal," Edward Burke, to run as her candidate for Cook County state's attorney. Charles Swibel remained in control of public housing and became an intimate and a top adviser. She brought Alderman Thomas Keane out of the retirement that followed his federal conviction, to redraw the Chicago ward map.

In one thing Byrne broke with Machine tradition. She remained as avid as ever for personal publicity and media attention. She hired ex-newspapermen as her top aides. By making unexpected offhand announcements, she encouraged reporters to trail behind her throughout every minute of every day. The reporters took to calling these impromptu press conferences "gangbangs." She would get into long, boozy harangues at night on the phone with newspaper and television reporters she had a beef with. She had a key line she delivered over and over. Reminded of past inconsistencies on the frequent occasions when she broke old promises, she would say, "I've said this since Day One. . . ." The line became as characteristic as Richard Nixon's famous one, "Let me make one thing perfectly clear."

Byrne's intense awareness of the news media was more than a quirk. It represented her recognition that times were a-changing. Although she strove to control the old Machine structure, handing out jobs and favors or threatening to punish enemies like any old-time boss—she once said of a political opponent who held city contracts that she would "cut his hands off" by taking away the city business—she knew it was not enough any more. In the old days, when things began to change after World War II, Jake Arvey and the boys had talked scornfully yet apprehensively about the "newspaper wards"—the wards that could be more affected by publicity than by the old ways of the precinct organizer with his favors and jobs and offers of friendship. Now the whole city paid heed to the six o'clock news, and Jane Byrne knew it.

"Television is the new precinct captain," she would announce on those days when she felt like resuming her anti-Machine election stance. Her preoccupation with the news media became a reliance on a kind of demagogic personal appeal. The newspapers picked up on her wild shifts in policy and personal style. Editorial cartoonists invented new savage images to depict her—as a clown, as a madwoman. Her day-to-day changes were so remarkable that *Tribune* political editor Dick Ciccone invented a series of dialogues in which Jane talked to herself, "Good Jane" talking to "Bad Jane."

Byrne's view of herself as a new-style "media politician" who governed an old-style political Machine led to an astonishing preoccupation with collecting campaign money. It had never been a Machine tradition to spend money on advertising in elections. Mike Bilandic hadn't spent much more than a million dollars on his campaign. But now Jane Byrne started building up an incredible war chest totaling nearly $10 million—collected, as papers filed with the county clerk attested, from businesses and unions and workers who did business with the city.

Vrdolyak, Burke and Swibel moved in carefully to see if this new occupant of the mayor's office might serve them as well as Bilandic had. She was more lively than Bilandic, at least, and she had a short attention span. She needed someone to run things while she made headlines. Cautiously, the old Machine crowd gathered around to salvage what was left and to see if business could be done in the same old way.

The party's county chairman, George Dunne, had wryly accepted the primary results and anointed Jane Byrne with the party's support. A few years before, he had dismissed her from the party office Daley had endowed her with, making it quite clear he viewed her as an annoying grandstander. If his view of her had not changed, the necessity of dealing with her had. Dunne was a gracious man, on the edges of power now, and he had made his fortune by selling insurance through his connected insurance agency. Byrne entered an uneasy alliance with Dunne as caretaker of the party for two years, until Vrdolyak, seeing his chance, decided to get rid of Dunne and gain control of what was left of party patronage as chairman of the Cook County Democratic central committee.

Vrdolyak, who had had the sense to send Jane a $2,000 contribution check in the week following her primary victory, kept Jane Byrne on his side through four tumultuous years. He convinced her and some of her neophyte aides that he was a political manipulator of genius. He was smart, in fact, but sometimes he was smart in that way the British call "too clever by half." He made mistakes by making unnecessary enemies. And then there were the longstanding enemies, like the Daley family which had never forgiven Vrdolyak, Bilandic, Donovan or Burke for cutting them out of the picture after the old man's death.

Tom Donovan saw the way things were and quit to become

president of the Chicago Mercantile Exchange as soon as Byrne won the primary. Burke and Vrdolyak hung on, and they did well as bosses of the City Council. Burke, desperate for higher office as black families replaced his old-line white support in his South Side Fourteenth Ward, was set up to run for state's attorney against Republican Carey in 1982. But Burke lost to young Richard Daley, who beat the Machine his father had perfected. Everyone was beating the Machine now, even the old man's son.

(Burke ran a monumentally bad campaign. At one point, emphasizing his intention to crack down on rapists if elected to be Cook County's head law enforcer, he distributed thousands of police whistles to women's groups, urging women to "blow the whistle" if they were attacked.)

Daley ran for the office of county prosecutor because it had some jobs and to find some clout with which to oppose Jane Byrne and Ed Vrdolyak in the 1983 mayoral race. When he announced he would run against Byrne in late 1982, dazed supporters predicted that the Emerald City days of the Machine would return. Perhaps they could not understand how thoroughly the Machine had been beaten, again and again, by insiders and outsiders, and that there was no Machine any more, only an empty shell.

The careful "committeeman's letter" days of the "organization of friends and neighbors" were over. The union of white ethnics and black wards had been blasted apart. The powerful combine that ensured primary victories was finished. The courts, the changing nature of federal law, the changing expectations of blacks, the exodus of ethnics to the suburbs, the rise of the new and shining commercial core city—all had changed the political game in Chicago as it had in the other cities of the country. The myth of the Machine lingered because it was convenient—for political commentators and sentimental politicians—to have some fixed institution to blame or praise for the problems of the city. Reality came like a 3 A.M. nightmare in 1983, when it was all well and truly over.

19

Go Around, Come Around

THE MACHINE WAS FINISHED THE DAY THAT JANE BYRNE BEAT it in February 1979, with her cult of personality. The Machine did not work on issues or on cults. It worked because it had logic and numbers on its side, attributes it no longer had as it came time for another personality to take over from Jane Byrne.

Edward Banfield, the University of Chicago professor who wrote admiringly of the Machine, said in 1955 that "there are dangers in 'personality' politics, especially in a city highly charged with racial antagonisms. . . ."[1]

He meant Chicago.

The collapse of the Machine had left a sudden vacuum like

a black hole in the center of the Chicago political universe. Everything was imploding and no one knew how to stop it.

In 1947, Jake Arvey had convinced Ed Kelly not to try for another turn as mayor on the basis of a private poll he had conducted which showed Kelly could not win. Kelly asked around among his friends and they agreed. A sensible man and a product of a large, anonymous Machine, Kelly agreed to step down, for his own good and the good of the Machine he had served.

Not so with Jane Byrne. The ranks of the Machine grumbled against her. They saw the way it was with voters in their precincts. They did not want to lose this great thing that had run the city for so long for the sake of a mercurial woman in City Hall who really didn't understand Machine politics at all.

The polls in late 1982 showed that Richard M. Daley was a thirty-point favorite over Jane Byrne in the coming primary. Jane could not believe it; she could not believe people did not love her. Instead, she decided the polls might be wrong if she changed and became "Good Jane" again.

She hired David Sawyer, a New York media adviser who became something of an issue by his mere presence in an insular Chicago campaign. Vague mutterings about New York "outsiders" dogged his steps, but Sawyer did a credible job. He held "focus sessions" in which groups of ordinary people talked about their perception of Jane Byrne. Jane saw the tapes of the sessions, shuddered and did what David Sawyer told her to do. She had to change her level of rhetoric, her dress, the way she walked and talked. She turned from "Fighting Jane" to "Executive Jane," a latter-day Anton Cermak changing her spots.

The change worked. By January, six weeks before the late February primary, Jane was beginning to look like a winner again. She was a master of television. Her opponent, Daley, was not. Like his father, he was shy, a wooden speaker, a stumbler and mumbler. He looked stupid on television and sort of punkish. What had been charming in his father was insipid in the son.

In such a situation, the black vote could be crucial, as it had been to Richard Senior back in 1955. But there was no Bill Dawson to bring the black vote home for Richard M. Instead, the blacks had their own man, Harold Washington, a product of the Dawson Machine.

Harold Washington had run for mayor against Bilandic in 1977 and had lost. He didn't have much guts for running again. He had landed a job as Congressman from the Black Belt and he liked the life of a legislator (which he had been for years as a Machine underling in Springfield).

But the black community—which included a number of rich and successful businessmen—raised the upfront money and a pledge for more, and Washington was enticed to go for it.

Harold Washington was a cold, casually indifferent man who could be a forceful speaker when he tried and who had a cutting edge to him. He was careless and lazy. He had no time for details. Friends and co-workers remembered him as always late. A bachelor, he balanced his checkbook in mornings over coffee in a shop on Hyde Park Boulevard down the street from his apartment.

He also had a disregard for the law bred in any number of Machine men, white and black, and particularly in the Dawson Machine. In 1972, he was convicted of failing to file federal income tax returns for four years. He explained in court that it had slipped his mind—an especially strange explanation since his birthday is on April 15. He served forty days in county jail, in the federal tier.

A few years before, in 1969, Washington apparently agreed

to handle divorces and other minor matters for five clients who later filed complaints that he took their down payments— a piddling total of $265 in all—and did nothing about them. The Chicago Bar Association asked for an explanation; usually, once it gets an explanation, it does nothing, but Washington never got around to explaining and when a couple of years passed, his law license was suspended.

This singular man whose best friend at the time was Clarence McClain, a convicted pimp whom he made his legislative assistant, was the great hope of the black community. At first, neither Jane nor Richard noticed him; Harold had been around too long, taking the Machine line in Springfield, arguing in long convoluted sentences about whites and blacks, practicing the intense racism so endemic to politicians white and black in the Machine: If something good happened to him, it was a victory for The People; if something bad happened, it was because of the White Man denying rights to The People. (The reverse worked as well for some whites).

For some strange reason, all three candidates agreed to television debates. Because of his weak style, Richie Daley had the most to lose, but he had to find some way to overcome the $10 million campaign chest accumulated by Jane Byrne's systematic shakedowns over four years of "financial" dealings with city contractors and suppliers.

There had never been television debates in Chicago politics before 1983. The Machine sold its candidates through the Machine; why give the opposition a chance at a free audience? But Byrne was sure she was right for the cameras—she had beaten Bilandic with television—and Washington, who spent little money on TV, saw no harm in it. Daley had to agree or look bad.

The debates were depressing. Richard Daley was as bad as everyone thought he would be. He "desed" and "dozed" his way through a jungle of syntax, hacking at the words with a machete delivery.

Jane Byrne was "Good Jane" for the most part, as cool as a cucumber as she invented statistics on the spur of the moment to show the good she had done for the city.

And Harold Washington?

"He didn't come off as a baboon," said one amazed city worker who was white and cheering for Daley.

He was, in fact, witty, reasonable, personable. Harold Washington gained credibility in the encounters. As the weeks passed, Washington's weaknesses were turned into selling points: to point out that Harold was a convicted felon and disbarred lawyer was somehow "racist." White liberals retreated into their lakefront enclaves to consider what they would do.

What they would do was split their votes—and what whites as a group citywide would do was split between Daley and Byrne, with Byrne slightly ahead. And what blacks did was turn it on for Washington, in every precinct in every black ghetto ward and in every well-off black ward.

Washington's approach was like that of the Irish factions before Sullivan and the Hinky Dinks and Bathhouse Johns. To hell with the Machine. Grab as much as you can as fast as you can and for as long as you can. Discipline in politics was a thing of the past. "It's our turn!" Washington cried to cheering throngs. On election night, a sudden Washington convert, Jesse L. Jackson, literally screamed at the TV cameras: "We want it alllllll now!"

Washington had rhetorical skills no Daley or Cermak had ever had. He beat up whitey in the black churches where he preached his political message: "We've been pushed around, shoved around, beat, murdered, emasculated, literally destroyed! But through it all, we've stayed together!"

Like the long-ago Oscar DePriest, Washington had always been a "race man." In 1983, he waved the bloody flag of racism for political edge and it worked. He did not have the Dawson touch, to build a machine, to put together the coherent numbers. It was not what he wanted, not what he was interested in. The press arrested his attention: It was "scurrilous" and "racist." He would not compromise with the Machine; the Machine was dead.

He was as manic as Jane Byrne. They were a pair of Robespierres, colliding in different revolutions. Neither could talk compromise or the language of accommodation; it was too late for that in Chicago.

Vrdolyak was driven to panic by what he saw in the numbers in the days before the election. He exhorted his workers to make their stand at Rourke's Drift against the Zulus: "A vote for Daley is a vote for Washington! It's a two-person race! It would be the worst day in the history of Chicago if your candidate, the only viable candidate, was not elected. It's a racial thing! Don't kid yourself! I'm calling on you to save your city, to save your precinct! We're fighting to keep the city the way it is!"[2]

Too late for words. Washington got 37 percent of the vote, 33 went to Byrne, and 30 to Daley.

THE REPUBLICANS HAD PUT UP THEIR USUAL TOKEN CANDIDATE in the primary. Bernard Epton from Hyde Park had the manner of an offended ostrich. He had been a Hyde Park liberal Republican in the state legislature for a time and he was a decent man.

The victory of Washington turned eyes on Epton, and the Republicans kicked themselves for not putting up a more viable candidate. Bernard did his best and his campaign echoed with vague race themes urging votes "before it's too late." Democratic committeemen such as Ed Kelly supported him openly; others did it quietly. Machine discipline was a shambles. Despite this, Epton nearly won, but an incredible 99 percent of the black vote went to Harold Washington, and he edged his way into office.

The election of 1983 only affirmed what had really happened to the Machine in 1979. There was no Machine, only Machine politicians who could not understand that their day was over. The city was polarized again as it had been in the old boodle days of Hinky Dink and "our Carter." It was every man and every ward for himself. The precinct captain did not matter any more; loyalty did not matter; your committeeman's letter was worthless. The chaos expected if the Machine ever broke apart came, and still everyone was amazed.

20
Third City

L OS ANGELES OFFICIALLY OUTSTRIPPED CHICAGO IN POPULA-
tion in the first year of the Washington administration.
Second City became Third and there were big headlines in
all the newspapers. Jazztime and Ragtime became Blues-
time. At least, that is what the politicians thought.

Harold Washington sounded the theme of his administration in the inaugural speech in which he challenged the Democratic regulars who had presided over the decline of the
Machine. He announced he would not cooperate with City
Council leaders like Ed Vrdolyak and Eddie Burke and that
he expected complete support from any and all black committeemen and aldermen who expected to stay on the good

side of the black community. He was doing no more than becoming a boss and using racial confrontation to do it. Washington remained lazy in administrative matters and bored by details. There was no ready-made cadre of Machine-trained operatives to handle the ins and outs of Chicago's extremely complex and fragmented governmental system for him. Because blacks had been out of power for so long and Washington had no intention of heading an administration run by whites, he found himself relying on neophytes who were more schooled in race rhetoric than in administrative reality. They were frequently outmaneuvered by the remnants of the old Machine.

The hard-working Vrdolyak quickly patched together a Council majority between the mayor's inaugural in May 1983 and the first City Council meeting. At that meeting, Vrdolyak stunned the press and fellow regulars by showing a 29 to 21 majority. He put his loyalists in at key committee posts and froze out the Washington minority. The confrontation satirized in the city's nightclub acts as "Council Wars" (after the Star Wars movies) had begun between Harold "Skywalker" and "Darth" Vrdolyak.

Because he was frozen by the Shakman decrees on patronage hiring and firing, Washington had a limited amount of room in which to maneuver. He pushed for a host of top-level appointments to such places as the library board, the Park District, the CTA board and the Chicago Housing Authority board, but most of them were bottled up for years in committee. Vrdolyak was fighting a slow, scorched-earth warfare against Washington, and Washington was content to let the fight drag on.

One of the Washington appointments that sailed through the Council was Renault Robinson's appointment as new executive director of the housing authority. Like Washington,

Robinson was a "race man" who fed on confrontation and headlines—except now the rhetoric could be turned into action. Unfortunately, Robinson simply did not know what to do with power.

He announced one day that the problems of the high-rise projects were caused by elevator repair crews (mostly white) sabotaging the elevator systems. He fired the company contracted to fix the elevators and fired the crews. Within days, elevators began to break down and no one knew how to fix them. One overweight mother died of a heart attack trying to climb fourteen flights of stairs back to her apartment. Washington was embarrassed to find blacks marching on his City Hall, blaming him for the mess in the projects.

The reaction of Chicagoans both to the racism spilled by their leaders in the 1983 campaign and the subsequent, race-baiting confrontations that followed in the Council and at the press conferences was curiously muted. A cynicism based on weariness with the antics of the decade of politics after Daley's death seemed to grip the ordinary people of the city. It was not a nice thing to see. The jokes about politics had that bitter edge celebrated in stories about the cabarets of prewar Berlin.

The rest of Third City thrived. The building boom on the lakefront begun during the Daley years surged on, oblivious to the conflicts in City Hall. Chicago theater was never better or more varied. Even the empty small factory buildings that ringed the Loop were suddenly converted into neighborhoods of trendy loft apartments.

What was happening in politics was not seen at first by the participants or paid observers in the press. The word "machine" was still bandied though there was no machine anymore. Perhaps Washington understood. He said, "The

Machine is dead, buried, finished." (His rhetoric ran in series of threes.)

Washington moved to award contracts to minority firms— usually black firms. When the city did not have enough minority firms to handle a certain contract, he used minority firms from places like Atlanta. His goal, he said, was to make certain that at least 30 percent of all contracts between the city and private firms were in the hands of minority-owned firms.

This was the one area left for him to maneuver in—to turn the flow of contract monies from traditional sources with ties to the remnants of the Machine and create new pools of wealth for his supporters.

No Shakman decrees prevailed here—and the Vrdolyak wing of the party was largely incapable of stopping it because minority participation in government business was the rule of the federal government. A federal investigation conducted by the FBI of abuses in local government revealed that in 1985 and 1986, aldermen backing the Washington administration were taking favors and cash to "grease" business introductions to the administration.

Washington's old friend Clarence McClain was one of the early casualties of the investigation of the kind of people Washington was bringing into government. McClain was revealed to be a convicted pimp, and he left city government though his name continued to surface as influential with the Washington administration. Washington denounced all attacks upon himself as being "racist" but after a while the word did not have meaning anymore. Chicagoans, accustomed to living on the racial edge, felt disgusted by both Vrdolyak and Washington.

Government in Chicago had become a series of games of

"chicken": When Washington wanted Council approval of a real estate tax hike to balance the budget, for instance, he had to threaten to fire 70,000 city workers—including, he warned to the noisy delight of his opponents, his own press secretary. The aldermen, threatened with the loss of their own jobs, caved in. It would happen over and over.

And things changed, and the changes seemed to go in Washington's favor. Though his popularity among whites never seemed to go up, his hold on the black community that had elected him never wavered. It was ironic that the Machine had itself set up a situation in which political control of blacks had become easier than political control of whites. Because of the Machine's policy of nonintegration in housing—a policy that reflected the wishes of both the white majority and such old black machine bosses as Bill Dawson—the black wards remained concentrated in political power long after the traditional white ethnic "river wards" had declined. The city lost nearly 600,000 middle-class residents to the suburbs between 1950 and 1980—and a significant majority were whites. Blacks were united in the face of divided white opposition, and they stayed united behind Washington.

The constant confrontation ground at the city's soul and puzzled outsiders. At the Democratic National Convention in 1984, a smiling television reporter tried, in a fit of ambition to be seen as a peacemaker, to get Washington and Vrdolyak to discuss the problem of Chicago. Washington refused and lashed out at the reporter, accusing him of scurrilous conduct. His outburst shocked the national press, but it was old stuff in Chicago.

The Machine could not deliver; therefore, there was no Machine.

A stunning example came when Adlai E. Stevenson III (son of the man who had helped shore up the Machine in 1948) decided to make a second try at becoming Illinois's governor in 1986. Stevenson was an indifferent campaigner but, like his father, he counted on the Machine to pull him through. Stevenson faced James Thompson, running for a fourth term, and was considered a good bet. But it was in the Democratic primary, that old bastion of Machine control, that Stevenson lost it all. Two bizarre nominees won slating as lieutenant governor and secretary of state on the Democratic ticket. They were disciples of the right-wing extremist Lyndon LaRouche. (Both had WASP-sounding names and their regular Democratic opponents had ethnic last names. The LaRouche candidates did extremely well both outside Chicago and in Chicago black wards—the day of ethnic politics and tickets balanced with ethnic, racial and religious divisions to attract the old coalition voters was over in the city.)

Stevenson blamed the public and the press for the turn of events. He would have been wiser to blame a political organization so lacking in discipline that the expected "Machine vote" out of Chicago no longer existed. Washington had not campaigned for Stevenson—though he did not oppose him, appearing rather indifferent to any contest that did not involve a direct run-in with the Vrdolyak forces—and Vrdolyak was so busy planning strategy for Council wars that the primary did not seem to hold much interest for him. If people from the old liberal, upper-class wing of the party, like Stevenson, were going to be in politics now—well, they would just have to go out and create their own, individual organization. There was no Machine to do it for them anymore.

Ironically, Stevenson formed a third-party candidacy under the banner of a hastily thrown together Solidarity party— he refused to run with the LaRouche candidates—and named Mike Howlett, Jr., the son of a Machine man his father had disliked, as his running mate.

Stevenson lost the November election to Thompson, but the ironies of a third-party bid supported by fragments of the old regular party remained. Because the Solidarity party did so well in total vote terms in November, it became a new, registered and recognized political party in Illinois. In the Illinois of Machine days, independent parties and candidates were discouraged by a web of election laws making it difficult to get on the ballot. Now the Stevenson wing of the dismembered Machine made further rending of the party possible.

The chairman of the Democratic Cook County Central Committee—the nominal "Machine" boss, Ed Vrdolyak—announced in December he would run for mayor in 1987 as either a Democrat or as the Solidarity party candidate and would not ask to be slated by the central committee he headed.

Jane Byrne, running as a maverick in the Democratic primary against Washington, said she would not seek the endorsement of the party either.

Washington, the Democratic mayor, said he would probably run again as a Democrat but he might form his own third party to run against the political organization he belonged to.

At this point, the weak Daley wing of the party developed its own candidate—the cool, competent boss of the Southwest Side and Cook County real estate assessor, Thomas Hynes. Hynes announced he would run as a Democrat but he might pull out before the primary and run against Washington as the Chicago First party mayoral candidate. Hynes was popular but his base was small. However, as the man whose office calculates the real estate tax, he had a big campaign chest and was on the air in early December with commercials urging Chicago to elect him as a healer of the city's political wounds.

This chaotic December of local politics marked the tenth anniversary of Daley's death. All the political warriors paused one bright afternoon to pay tribute to the last boss of the last

Machine. Even Washington spoke, in the City Council tribute, of Daley's love for the city. Daley's sons were on the Council dais beneath an immense portrait of the man. How it had all changed in one decade. They all said great words about the man they called the Late Mayor—as if he had just stepped into eternity the day before—and when the words were done, they went back to the business of tearing the remnants of the party apart.

The confused race for mayor and the hundreds of candidates who filed in 1986 to run for the various City Council posts perhaps reflected more than the death of the Last Machine. It reflected a new reality for Chicago and other big cities in the country. The cities had formed the spine of the Democratic coalition. In the great days of the cities, mayors talked to presidents and aid for social projects concentrated in cities—housing, education, welfare, health care—came directly through city machines.

Now a decade of Carter and Reagan had broken the old binding ties between cities and federal agencies. The new powers were state governors, from Cuomo to Thompson. The state houses in those states dominated by large cities reasserted themselves.

The age of the city machine passed. It happened sooner in New York, Boston and Philadelphia than Chicago. This was largely because of the zestful Machine reformer Jack Arvey, who bought the Machine a second chance through his wise maneuverings, and of Richard Daley, whose singular genius in the art of governing held together the illusion the Machine offered. It was an illusion of unity, strength and competence. There were always people who knew it was only an illusion, but even some of the critics said that good politics was always a matter of illusion.

Daley was the great Oz of Chicago, working the fire and

wind Machine from a booth behind the curtain at City Hall.
And when the truth was discovered—that Oz was mortal and
so was the Machine—the shattered illusion was not a good
thing to see. Chicago, approaching the last years of the century it began with such boastful enthusiasm, slouched a little.
Maybe that is what reality—political reality—does to cities.

Notes

PROLOGUE: **THE CENTER DOES NOT HOLD**

1. Remark attributed to George Dunne by the late Lynn Williams, New Trier township committeeman, during a 1979 interview.

ONE: **THE CITY ALONE**

1. For an analysis of the impoverished Irish diet and its consequences, see Cecil Woodham-Smith, *The Great Hunger* (New York: Harper & Row, 1963).
2. *Chicago Tribune,* April 19, 1874.
3. Ibid., July 27, 1868.

TWO: **RAGTIME**

1. Ben Hecht, *Gaily, Gaily* (Garden City, N.Y.: Doubleday, 1963), pp. 210–11.

2. Ibid., p. 213.

3. Ibid.

4. *Chicago Tribune,* June 6, 1911.

5. Quoted in Charles Fanning, *Finley Peter Dunne and Mr. Dooley, The Chicago Years* (Lexington, Ky.: University of Kentucky Press, 1978), p. 125.

THREE: **THE GAS MAN**

1. Paul M. Green, *The Chicago Democratic Party 1840–1920: From Factionalism to Political Organization,* Ph.D. Thesis, University of Chicago, Department of History, 1975.

2. Milton L. Rakove, *We Don't Want Nobody Nobody Sent, an Oral History of the Daley Years* (Bloomington, Ind.: Indiana University Press, 1979).

FOUR: **THE DEMAGOGUE OF PRAIRIE AVENUE**

1. Lloyd Wendt and Herman Kogan, *Big Bill of Chicago* (New York: Bobbs-Merrill, 1953), p. 107.

2. Charles Merriam, *Chicago* (New York: Macmillan, 1927), p. 146.

4. Wendt and Kogan, op. cit., p. 121.

FIVE: **JAZZTIME**

1. Jay Robert Nash, *People to See: An Anecdotal History of Chicago's Makers and Breakers* (Piscataway, N.J.: New Century Publishers, Inc., 1981), p. 87.

2. Ibid., p. 86.

3. Paul M. Green, *The Chicago Democratic Party 1840–1920,* Ph.D. Thesis, University of Chicago, Department of History, 1975, p. 273.

4. Ibid., pp. 284–85.

5. *Chicago Sun-Times* and *Chicago Tribune,* February 21, 1983.

6. Lloyd Wendt and Herman Kogan, *Big Bill of Chicago* (Indianapolis, Ind.: Bobbs-Merrill, 1953), p. 260.

7. Ibid., p. 263.

8. Ibid., p. 261.

9. Ibid., pp. 225–28.

SIX: PUSHCART

1. Alex Gottfried, *Boss Cermak of Chicago: A Study of Political Leadership* (Seattle, Wash.: University of Washington Press, 1962), p. 13.
2. Ibid., p. 14
3. Ibid., p. 29.

SEVEN: WET STUFF

1. Alex Gottfried, *Boss Cermak of Chicago: A Study of Political Leadership* (Seattle, Wash.: University of Washington Press, 1962), pp. 50–51.
2. Ibid., p. 78.
3. Ibid., p. 115.
4. Ibid.
5. Ibid.
6. Ibid., p. 117.
7. Ibid., p. 126.
8. Ibid., pp. 125–26.
9. Len O'Connor, *Clout: Mayor Daley and His City* (Chicago: Henry Regnery Company, 1975), p. 42.
10. *Chicago Herald & Examiner,* March 17, 1934.
11. James Winters, "Democracy in Chicago," *Notre Dame Magazine,* December 1983.

EIGHT: MACHINE

1. Alex Gottfried, *Boss Cermak of Chicago: A Study of Political Leadership* (Seattle, Wash.: University of Washington Press, 1962), p. 120.
2. "An Appeal to Reason," Rev. Alonzo J. Bowling, political editor of the *Chicago Review,* pamphlet.
3. Gottfried, op. cit., p. 220.
4. Ibid., p. 223.
5. Milton L. Rakove, *We Don't Want Nobody Nobody Sent* (Bloomington, Ind.: Indiana University Press, 1979), p. 32.
6. Gottfried, op. cit., p. 134.
7. *Chicago Tribune,* October 11, 1931.

8. "Democracy in Chicago," James Winters, *Notre Dame Magazine,*
December 1983, p. 15.
9. Headline in the *Chicago Examiner,* February 16, 1933.
10. Gottfried, op. cit., p. 326.

NINE: **THE CASH MACHINE**

1. *Chicago Tribune,* March 11, 1936.
2. Gwen Morgan and Arthur Veysey, *Poor Little Rich Boy* (Wheaton,
Il.: The DuPage Heritage Gallery, 1983), pp. 88–89.
3. Elmer Lynn Williams, "The Fixit Boys: The Insider Story of the
New Deal and the Kelly-Nash Machine," self-published pamphlet,
1940.
4. Channel Two News investigation, 1981.
5. H. Dicken Cherry, "Effective Precinct Organization," unpub-
lished dissertation (Chicago: University of Chicago, Department of
Political Science, 1952), p. 70.
6. Ibid.
7. Milton L. Rakove, *We Don't Want Nobody Nobody Sent* (Bloomington, Ind.: Indiana University Press, 1979), p. 26.
8. ———, *Don't Make No Waves, Don't Back No Losers* (Bloomington,
Ind.: Indiana University Press, 1975), pp. 112–13.
9. Cherry, op. cit., p. 70.
10. A. J. Liebling, *Chicago: The Second City* (New York: Alfred A.
Knopf, 1952), pp. 122–24.
11. William T. Stead, *If Christ Came to Chicago!* (Chicago: Laird and
Lee, 1894), p. 59.
12. Quoted in Charles Fanning, *Finley Peter Dunne and Mr. Dooley*
(Lexington, Ky.: University Press of Kentucky, 1978).

TEN: **THE OTHER BIG BILL**

1. *Chicago Tribune,* April 5, 1932.
2. Vernon Jarrett, "William L. Dawson: A Look at 'The Man,' "
Chicago Tribune, February 25, 1970.
3. Ibid.
4. Ibid.
5. Harold Gosnell, *Negro Politicians: The Rise of Negro Politics in*

Chicago (Chicago: University of Chicago Press, 1935, reprinted 1967), p. 124.

6. Ibid.

7. Dempsey Travis, *An Autobiography of Black Chicago* (Chicago: Urban Research Institute, 1981), p. 41.

8. Gosnell, op. cit., pp. 124–25.

9. Vernon Jarrett, "An Old Pro Views Political Strategy," *Chicago Tribune*, February 8, 1974.

10. Gosnell, op. cit., p. 134.

ELEVEN: **SECOND CITY**

1. A. J. Liebling, *Chicago: The Second City* (New York: Alfred A. Knopf, 1952), p. 44.

2. Milton L. Rakove, *We Don't Want Nobody Nobody Sent* (Bloomington, Ind.: Indiana University Press, 1979), p. 6.

3. Stanley Frankel, "Arvey of Illinois: New-Style Political Boss," *Collier's*, July 23, 1949, p. 52.

4. Paul H. Douglas, *In the Fullness of Time* (New York: Harcourt, Brace, Jovanovich, 1971), p. 91.

5. Ibid., p. 92.

6. Ibid., p. 91.

7. Ralph Berkowitz, interview, 1973.

8. Ibid.

9. Quoted in James Winters, "Democracy in Chicago," *Notre Dame Magazine*, December 1983, p. 17.

10. Ibid.

11. Ibid.

12. Ibid.

13. Ralph Berkowitz, interview, 1973.

14. John Bartlow Martin, *Adlai Stevenson of Illinois* (New York: Doubleday & Co., 1976), p. 267.

15. Rakove, op. cit., p. 11.

16. Martin, op. cit., p. 280.

TWELVE: **IN BLACK AND WHITE**

1. Philip M. Hauser and Evelyn M. Kitagawa, *Local Community Fact Book for Chicago 1950* (Chicago: University of Chicago, 1953), p. 2.

2. Dempsey Travis, *An Autobiography of Black Chicago* (Chicago: Urban Research Institute), p. 54.

3. Martin Meyerson and Edward C. Banfield, *Politics, Planning and the Public Interest* (New York: The Free Press, 1964), p. 85.

4. Ibid., p. 140.

5. Ibid., pp. 20–21.

6. Ibid., p. 199.

7. William Mullen, "The Road to Hell," *Chicago Tribune Sunday Magazine,* March 31, 1985, p. 16.

8. "Council OK's Group to Probe Racial Strife," *Chicago Tribune,* October 15, 1953.

9. "Board Fires Miss Wood in CHA Dispute," *Chicago Tribune,* September 4, 1954.

THIRTEEN: **DALEY**

1. John Bartlow Martin, *Adlai Stevenson of Illinois* (New York: Doubleday & Company, Inc., 1976), p. 359.

2. Quoted in Martin, p. 359.

3. Len O'Connor, *Clout: Mayor Daley and His City* (Chicago: Henry Regnery Co., 1975), p. 72.

4. Ibid.

5. Ibid., p. 80.

6. Ibid.

7. Quoted in James Winters, "Democracy in Chicago," *Notre Dame Magazine,* December 1983, p. 18.

FOURTEEN: **BROTHERS' BOY**

1. James Winters, "Democracy in Chicago," *Notre Dame Magazine,* December 1983, pp. 17–18.

2. Len O'Connor, *Clout: Mayor Daley and His City* (Chicago: Henry Regnery Co., 1975), p. 113.

3. Winters, op. cit., p. 18.

4. Ralph Berkowitz, interview, 1973.

5. Edward C. Banfield, *Political Influence* (New York: The Free Press, 1961), pp. 270–72.

6. Eugene Kennedy, *Himself! The Life and Times of Mayor Richard J. Daley* (New York: Viking Press, 1978), p. 78.

FIFTEEN: CRACKS, REFORMS

1. Milton L. Rakove, *Don't Make No Waves, Don't Back No Losers* (Bloomington, Ind.: University of Indiana Press, 1975), pp. 112–13.

SIXTEEN: AFTER THE END

1. Milton L. Rakove, *Don't Make No Waves, Don't Back No Losers* (Bloomington, Ind.: University of Indiana Press, 1975), p. 83.

SEVENTEEN: FIGHTING JANE

1. Eleanor Randolph, "Conflict of Interest: A Growing Problem for Couples," *Esquire* 89:5509, February 1978.
2. *Chicago Tribune,* February 15, 1979.

NINETEEN: GO AROUND, COME AROUND

1. Edward C. Banfield, *Political Influence* (New York: The Free Press, 1961), p. 259.
2. *Chicago Sun-Times* and *Chicago Tribune,* February 21, 1983.

Index

BILL GRANGER was born and raised in Chicago. He went to De LaSalle Institute and DePaul University, where he majored in English. He was named to *Who's Who in American Colleges and Universities* while at DePaul. His first newspaper job was as a copyboy at the *Chicago Daily News*. He left college in his senior year to work for United Press International. He served two years in the Army and after service joined the staff of the *Chicago Tribune* in 1966. He helped cover the racial riots in Chicago in the 1960s and the violence surrounding the Democratic National Convention in 1968. The following year, he joined the *Chicago Sun-Times*. He wrote about crime, politics and social trends and, in 1978, began to write novels. He has published fourteen novels. One of his novels, *Public Murders,* won the Mystery Writers of America award, the Edgar, in 1980. His novels have been translated into thirteen languages. He has reported from Chicago, across the United States, and in Europe. He has contributed to *The New Republic, Reader's Digest, Time, The New York Times, The Washington Post, Newsday,* the *Columbia Journalism Review* and other journals. Once asked by Mayor Richard Daley where he went to high school, he mentioned the mayor's own school; when asked where he went to college, he mentioned the mayor's college. The late mayor then asked: "You went to De LaSalle and DePaul and you ended up writing for newspapers? Where the hell did you go wrong?" Since 1980, he has contributed a column to the *Chicago Sunday Tribune* and he is listed in *Who's Who in America.*

LORI GRANGER grew up in Chicago and Washington, D.C. She received her B.A. from Antioch College (Yellow Springs, Ohio). She received her M.A., specializing in inner-city political science, from Roosevelt University, Chicago. She studied as a fellow of the National Opinion Research Center, Chicago, and as a doctoral candidate in political science at the University of Chicago. She was an editor at the *Day Papers* in suburban Chicago. She operated her own news syndicate, specializing in government and political news, called Central News of Chicago. She has taught political science at the Illinois Institute of Technology and DePaul University. She has worked on the election staffs of Republicans and Democrats: Adlai E. Stevenson III, the late Senator Paul Douglas and Bernard Carey, who became public prosecutor in Cook County on a reform ticket. With her husband, she is coauthor of *Fighting Jane,* a study of Mayor Jane Byrne of Chicago, published by Dial Press; and *The Magic Feather,* a critical study of special education, published by E. P. Dutton.

The authors are married, have a son and do not tell each other whom they vote for.